THE STORY
OF THE OTHER WISE MAN

This is a change of pace for Wayne Frye that will keep the reader mesmerized with a different kind of mystery and intrigue that will titillate the senses and motivate deep spiritual thoughts.

Most people know the story of the *Three Wise Men of the East*, and how they travelled from far away to offer their gifts at the manger in Bethlehem. But how many have heard the story of the other wise man, who also saw the star on its rising and set out to follow it? Yet, he did not arrive with his brethren to worship the young child, Jesus.

Of the great desire of this fourth pilgrim to see Jesus, and how it was denied, yet remarkably accomplished in the denial, of his many wanderings and the probations of his soul, of the long way of his seeking, and the strange way of his finding the one whom he sought is the story told herein. It is a tale from fragments of the Hall of Dreams in the palace of the heart of mankind.

The Legend
Of the Fourth Wise Man

J. Wayne Frye

This book is written in Canadian English

The Legend of the Fourth Wise Man

J. Wayne Frye

The Legend of the Fourth Wise Man

To: Barbara O'Brien
Thanks for the years that we shared the joy of
rearing three wonderful children.
And as always to my muse,
Lynton Viñas Frye.
And to good old Henry – my impetus & guide

Catalogue Number: 8341-945-918-20248
ISBN: 978-1-928183-74-7

Fireside Books
&
Peninsula Publishing

J. Wayne Frye

The Legend of the Fourth Wise Man

The Legend of the Fourth Wise Man

J. Wayne Frye

The Legend of the Fourth Wise Man

The Legend of the Fourth Wise Man

Prologue
That Ain't My Kinda God

Who seeks for atonement alone to save the soul
May keep the path, but will not reach the goal;
While he who walks in love may wander far,
They will be brought to where the blessed are.

Evil is too often promoted by charlatans
Who point the finger of condemnation,
Rather than offering the hand of acceptance.
This is the hypocrisy of religion.

Just look at the cult of MAGA,
Worshipping that buffoon Donald Trump,
Who represents everything that

J. Wayne Frye

The Legend of the Fourth Wise Man

Jesus warned against in sermon after sermon.

Hypocrisy is the bane of religion,
As it drives truly caring people away,
Making a mockery of truth and faith
In a world ruled by greed.

Sometimes it takes an irreligious individual to weave a harrowing tale of how faith and dedication can elevate a person to heights of grandeur in the glorification of true faith. I am a person who is appalled at how religion is used as a manipulative tool to promote true evil. In fact, I once had a Catholic priest tell me that some of the kindness people he knew were atheists and some of the cruellest were Christians. What a damning indictment of religion by a person who is a servant of God. All one has to do is look at many of the people in the MAGA movement in the so called Christian nation of the USA, and it is easy to see how evil is manifested in the guise of serving God and doing the work of Jesus.

It is said that good works do not get you into heaven. The belief that Jesus is the one and only true saviour is the assured ticket to heaven according to the Bible; consequently, no matter how many good deeds a person does they are of no use to a God who turns his back on those doing good deeds if they do not accept Christ as

The Legend of the Fourth Wise Man

their saviour. This God will admit a person like Adolph Hitler to heaven as long as he repents and accepts Jesus before he dies. This is the same God who killed the first born sons of Egypt when the Pharaoh refused to let the Jews flee the land. The first born had done no wrong, many being just born, but were still punished. This is the irony of those who profess belief. They willingly accept cruelty as a condition of being religious. I had a grandmother who was the kindest and most gracious individual I have ever known, but she had her doubts about religion. If she is not in heaven, it is not a place I want to go.

Additionally, my grandfather was a man of very few words, whom I have learned to appreciate more and more as I have aged and reflect back upon the great wisdom of an uneducated man with a great understanding of human nature. As we were sitting on his porch one Sunday, I asked him why he always just sat in the car while my grandmother went into church. He replied, "Well, first of all them there people in that church ain't offering me anything I need. The majority of them are hypocrites. They don't live what they preach. Religion is about fear, fear of retribution from God. Religion is used to control people. Ain't nobody gonna control your old granddaddy. I treat people with respect and kindness, and if that ain't enough to get you into heaven, it ain't no place I want to go."

It was then when I asked him, "What you really believe granddaddy?"

His reply, "I stopped believing in fairy tales, when I was about five years old. We all eventually stop believing in Santa Claus, but we still believing in this here Bible. Well, I ain't saying there weren't no Jesus, but I am saying that a person who leads a good life, is kind to others and tries to always do right should have a path to heaven, if there is such a place, even if he is a non-believer. What kinda God would punish a child who dies before adulthood, if he ain't never been exposed to Jesus. What kinda God would send a child to a fiery eternity in hell 'cause he don't believe what he ain't never heard of through no fault of his own. That ain't my kinda God."

The Legend of the Fourth Wise Man

Chapter 1
The King is Coming

Tradition cites three magi
visited the Christ Child
on that first Christmas
so serene, peaceful and mild,
but from the annals of old
another story is told
of a fourth wise man
courageous, loving and bold.

In the days when Augustus Caesar was master of many kings and Herod reigned in Jerusalem, there lived in the city of Ecbatana, among the mountains of Persia, a certain man named

The Legend of the Fourth Wise Man

Artimus, the Median. His house stood close to the outermost of the seven walls which encircled the royal treasury. From his roof he could look over the rising battlements of black and white, crimson, blue, red, silver and gold to the hill where the summer palace of the Parthian emperors glittered like a jewel in an anointed crown.

Around the dwelling of Artimus spread a garden, a tangle of flowers and fruit-trees, watered by a score of streams descending from the slopes of Mount Orontes and made musical by innumerable birds chirping all about. However, all colour was lost in the soft and odorous darkness of the late September night, and all sounds were hushed in the deep charm of silence, save the plashing of the water, like a voice half sobbing and half laughing under the shadows. High above the trees, a dim glow of light shone through the curtained arches of the upper chamber, where the master of the house was holding council with his friends.

He stood by the doorway to greet his guests. He was a tall, dark man of about forty years, with brilliant eyes sit near together under his broad brow, and firm lines graven around his fine, thin lips. He had the brow of a dreamer and the mouth of a soldier, a man of sensitive feeling but inflexible will, one of those who, in

The Legend of the Fourth Wise Man

whatever age they may live, are born for inward conflict and a life of service.

His flowing robe was not ostentatious by any stretch of the imagination. Yet, it was of pure white wool, thrown over a tunic of old well-worn silk; and he sported a white, pointed cap, with long lapels at the sides, resting on his flowing, gorgeous coal-black hair. It was the dress of an ancient priesthood, and all about him were other priests wearing the very finest of garments. These men were called the fire-worshippers, and each of them enjoyed their wealth. All except that is except Artimus, who was well known for being a modest man.

"Welcome!" he boldly said, in his low, pleasant, baritone voice, as one after another entered the room. "Welcome, Abdus; peace be with you, Rhodaspes and Tigranes, and with you my dear Abgarus. You are all welcome, and this house grows bright with the joy of your presence."

There were nine men, differing widely in age, but alike in the richness of their dress, except for Artimus, of many-coloured silks, and in the massive golden collars around their necks, marking them as Parthian nobles, and in the winged circles of gold resting upon their breasts the sign of the followers of Zoroaster.

The Legend of the Fourth Wise Man

These were all men of great wealth, and they showed it except for Artimus. His modesty stood in stark contrast to the rest, who took delight in displaying their immense wealth.

They took their places around a small black altar at the end of the room, where a tiny flame was burning. Artimus, standing beside it, fed the hearth with dry sticks of pine and fragrant oils. Then he began the ancient chant of the priesthood, and the voices of his companions joined in the beautiful hymn:

We worship the Spirit Divine,
All wisdom and goodness possessing,
Surrounded by Holy Immortals,
The givers of bounty and blessing.
We joy in the works of His hands,
His truth and His power confessing.

We praise all the things that are pure,
For these are His only Creation;
The thoughts that are true, and the words
And deeds that have won approbation;
These are supported by Him,
And for these we make adoration.

Hear us. Thou livest
In truth and in heavenly gladness;
Cleanse us from falsehood, and keep us
From evil and bondage to badness;

The Legend of the Fourth Wise Man

Pour out the light and the joy of Thy life
On our darkness and sadness.

Shine on our gardens and fields,
Shine on our working and weaving;
Shine on the whole race of man,
Believing and unbelieving;
Shine on us now through the night,
Shine on us now in Thy might.

The fire rose with the chant, throbbing as if it were a musical flame, until it cast illumination, revealing its simplicity and splendour.

The floor was laid with tiles of dark blue, veined with white; pilasters of twisted silver stood out against the blue walls; the clearstory of round-arched windows above them was hung with azure silk; the vaulted ceiling was a pavement of sapphires, like the body of heaven in its clearness, sown with silver stars. From the four corners of the roof hung four golden magic-wheels, called the tongues of the gods. At the one end, behind the altar, there were two dark-red pillars of hard rock containing crystals; above them a beam made of the same stone, on which was carved the figure of a winged archer.

The doorway between the pillars, which opened upon the simple terrace, was covered

The Legend of the Fourth Wise Man

with a heavy curtain of the colour of a ripe pomegranate, embroidered with innumerable golden rays shooting upward from the floor. In effect the room was like a quiet, starry night, all azure and silver, flushed with promise of the coming dawn. It represented the character and spirit of the master of the adobe.

He turned to his friends when the song was ended, and invited them to be seated. "You have come tonight," he said, looking around the circle, "at my calling, as faithful scholars to renew your worship and rekindle your faith in the God of Purity, even as this fire has been rekindled on the altar. We worship not the fire, but Him of whom it is the chosen symbol, because it is the purest of all created things. It speaks to us of one who is light and truth"

"Well said," answered the venerable Abgarus.

"The enlightened are never idolaters. They lift the veil of the form and go in to the shrine of reality, and new light and truth are coming to them continually through the old symbols."

"Hear me, then, my friends" said Artimus, very quietly, "while I tell you of the new light and truth that have come to me through the most ancient of all signs. We have searched the secrets of nature together, and studied the

The Legend of the Fourth Wise Man

healing virtues of water and fire. We have read also the books of prophecy in which the future was dimly foretold in words that are hard to understand. But the highest of all learning is the knowledge of the stars. To trace their courses is to untangle the threads of the mystery of life from the beginning to the end. If we could follow them perfectly, nothing would be hidden from us. But is not our knowledge of them still incomplete? Are there not many stars still beyond our horizon? Lights that are known only to the dwellers in the far away lands, among those across the desert."

There was a murmur of assent among the listeners. Murmurs of agreement that there was something mysterious about to happen.

"The stars," said Tigranes, "are the thoughts of the Eternal. They are numberless. But the thoughts of man can be counted, like the years of life. The wisdom of the Magi is the greatest of all wisdoms on earth, because it knows its own ignorance. And that is the secret of power. We keep men always looking and waiting for new sunrises. But we ourselves know that the darkness is equal to the light, and that the conflict between them will never be ended."

"That does not satisfy me," answered Artimus, "for, if the waiting must be endless, if there could be no fulfilment of it, then it would not be wise to look and wait. We should become like those new learners partaking of enlightenment, who say that there is no truth, and that the only wise men are those who spend their lives in discovering and exposing the lies that have been believed in the world. But the new sunrise will certainly dawn in the appointed time. Do not our own books tell us that this will come to pass, and that men will see the brightness of a great light?"

"That is true," said Abgarus; "every faithful disciple knows this and carries the word in his heart. In that day Sosiosh the Victorious shall arise out of the number of the prophets in the country to our west. Around him shall shine a mighty brightness, and he shall make life everlasting, incorruptible, immortal and the dead shall rise again."

"This is a dark saying," said Tigranes, "and it may be that we shall never understand it. It is better to consider the things that are near at hand, and to increase the influence of the Magi in their own country, rather than to look for one who may be a stranger, and to whom we must resign our power."

The others seemed to approve these words. There was a silent feeling of agreement

The Legend of the Fourth Wise Man

manifest among them; their looks responded with that indefinable expression which always follows when a speaker has uttered the thought that has been slumbering in the hearts of listeners. But Artimus turned to Abgarus with a glow on his face, and said, "I have kept this prophecy in the secret place of my soul. Religion without a great hope would be like an altar without a living fire. And now the flame has burned more brightly, and by the light of it I have read other words which also have come from the Fountain of Truth, and speak yet more clearly of the rising of the Victorious One in his brightness."

He drew from the breast of his tunic two small rolls of fine linen, with writing upon them, and unfolded them carefully upon his knee. "In the years that are lost in the past, long before our fathers came into the land of Babylon, there were wise men in Chaldea, from whom the first of the Magi learned the secret of the heavens. And of these Balaam, the son of Beor, was one of the mightiest. Hear the words of his prophecy: "There shall come a star out of the night, and a sceptre shall arise out of Israel.""

The lips of Tigranes drew downward with contempt, as he said, "Judah was a captive by the waters of Babylon, and the sons of Jacob were in bondage to our kings. The tribes of

The Legend of the Fourth Wise Man

Israel are scattered through the mountains like lost sheep, and from the remnant that dwells in Judea under the yoke of Rome neither star nor sceptre shall arise."

"And yet," answered Artimus, "it was the Hebrew Daniel, the mighty searcher of dreams, the counsellor of kings, the wise Belteshazzar, who was most honoured and beloved. He was a prophet of sure things and a reader of the thoughts of God. Daniel proved himself to our people. And he wrote to know, therefore, and understand that from the going forth of the commandment to restore Jerusalem, unto the Anointed One, the Prince, the time shall be seven and threescore and two weeks."

"But, said Abgarus, doubtfully, "these are mystical numbers. Who can interpret them, or who can find the key that shall unlock their meaning?"

Artimus answered: "It has been shown to me and to my three companions among the Magi—Caspar, Melchior and Balthazar. We have searched the ancient tablets of Chaldea and computed the time. It falls in this year. We have studied the sky, and in the spring of the year we saw two of the greatest stars draw near together. We also saw a new star there, which shone for one night and then vanished. Now

The Legend of the Fourth Wise Man

again the two great planets are meeting. This night is their conjunction. My three brothers are watching at the ancient temple in Babylonia, and I am watching here. If the star shines again, they will wait ten days for me at the temple, and then we will set out together for Jerusalem, to see and worship the promised one who shall be born King of Israel. I believe the sign will come. I have made ready for the journey. I have sold my house and my possessions, and bought these three jewels—a sapphire, a ruby and a pearl to carry them as tribute to the king. And I ask you to go with me on the pilgrimage that we may have joy together in finding the Prince who is worthy to be served."

While he was speaking, he thrust his hand into the inmost fold of his gown and drew out three great gems. One blue as a fragment of the night sky, one redder than a ray of sunrise and one as pure as the peak of a snow mountain at twilight. He laid them on the outspread linen scrolls before him.

But his friends looked on with strange and alien eyes. A veil of doubt and mistrust came over their faces, like a fog creeping up from the marshes to hide the hills. They glanced at each other with looks of wonder and pity, as those who have listened to incredible sayings, the

The Legend of the Fourth Wise Man

story of a wild vision or the proposal of an impossible enterprise.

At last Tigranes said: "Artimus, this is a vain dream. It comes from too much looking upon the stars and the cherishing of lofty thoughts. It would be wiser to spend the time in gathering money for the new temple. No king will ever rise from the broken race of Israel, and no end will ever come to the eternal strife of light and darkness. He who looks for it is a chaser of shadows. Farewell."

And another said: "Artimus, I have no knowledge of these things, and my office as guardian of the royal treasure binds me here. The quest is not for me. But if thou must follow it, fare thee well."

And another said: "In my house there sleeps a new bride, and I cannot leave her nor take her with me on this strange journey. This quest is not for me. But may thy steps be prospered wherever thou go. So, farewell."

And another said: "I am ill and unfit for hardship."

But Abgarus, the oldest and the one who loved Artimus the best, lingered after the others had gone, and said, gravely, "It may be

The Legend of the Fourth Wise Man

that the light of truth is in this sign that has appeared in the skies, and then it will surely lead to the Prince and the mighty brightness. Or it may be that it is only a shadow of the light, as Tigranes has said, and then he who follows it will have only a long pilgrimage and an empty search. But it is better to follow even the shadow of the best than to remain content with the worst. And those who would see wonderful things must often be ready to travel alone. I am too old for this journey, but my heart shall be a companion of the pilgrimage day and night, and I shall know the end of thy quest. Go in peace."

So, one by one, those remaining went out of the azure chamber and left Artimus in solitude. He gathered up the jewels and returned them to his gown. For a long time he stood and watched the flame that flickered and sank upon the altar. Then he crossed the hall, lifted the heavy curtain, and passed out between the dull red pillars to the terrace.

The shiver that thrills through the earth as it rouses from night sleep had already begun, and the cool wind that heralds the daybreak was drawing downward from the lofty snow-traced ravines of the mountains in the distance. Birds, half awakened, crept and chirped among the rustling leaves, and the smell of ripened crops came in brief wafts from the arbours.

The Legend of the Fourth Wise Man

Far over the eastern plain a white mist stretched like a soft blanket. But where the distant peaks serrated the western horizon, the sky was clear. Jupiter and Saturn rolled together like drops of lambent flame about to blend in one.

As Artimus watched them, an azure spark was born out of the darkness, rounding itself with purple splendours to a crimson sphere, and sparring upward through rays of orange into a point of white radiance. Tiny and infinitely remote, yet perfect in every part, it pulsated in the enormous vault, as if the three jewels in the Artimus' gown had mingled and been transformed into a living heart of light. He bowed his head. He covered his brow with his hands. "It is the sign," he said. "The King is coming, and I will go to meet him."

Chapter 2
It Is a Virtue

Artimus was his name, wisest of the wise.
Studying the sparkling stars. he surmised
In Judea the birth of a king so sublime,
Coming to a world so desperate at that time.

All night long Vasda, the swiftest of Artimus' vast array of camels, had been impatiently waiting for his master to mount him and ride into the desert, saddled and bridled, in her single stall, pawing the ground impatiently, while furiously shaking her bit as if she shared the eagerness of her master's purpose, though she knew not its meaning.

The Legend of the Fourth Wise Man

Before the birds had fully roused to their strong, high, joyful chant of morning song, before the white mist had begun to lift lazily from the plain, the fourth wise man was in the saddle, riding swiftly along the high-road, which skirted the base of the mountains nearby.

How close, how intimate the comradeship between a man and his favourite camel on a long, arduous journey of great importance. It was a silent, comprehensive friendship, an intercourse beyond the need of words. They drank at the same way-side springs and slept under the same guardian stars. They were conscious together of the subduing spell of nightfall and the quickening joy of daybreak. The master shared his evening meal with his hungry companion, and felt the soft, moist lips caressing the palm of his hand as they closed over the morsel of bread. In the grey dawn, Artimus was roused from his bed by the gentle stir of a warm breath over his sleeping face, and looked up into the eyes of his faithful fellow-traveller, ready and waiting for the toil of the day. Surely, unless he was a pagan and an unbeliever, by whatever name he called upon his God, he would thank him for this voiceless sympathy, this committed affection, and his morning prayer would embrace a double blessing for them both.!

The Legend of the Fourth Wise Man

And then, through the keen morning air, the swift hoofs beat their spirited music along the route, keeping time to the pulsing of two hearts that were moved with the same eager desire to conquer space, to devour the distance, to attain the goal of the journey in order to pay reverence to a new king.

Artimus rode wisely and well to keep the appointed hour with the other Magi; for the route was long and arduous, and the heat of the desert sun was tiring. But he knew Vasda's strength and pushed forward without anxiety, making a fixed distance every day, though he travelled late into the night, and was up in the morning long before sunrise as he passed along the brown slopes of mountains and dunes, furrowed by the course of weaving torrents of sand.

He crossed the level plains of the Nisaeans, where the famous herds of horses, feeding in the wide pastures, tossed their heads at Vasda's approach, and galloped away with a thunder of many hoofs. Flocks of wild birds rose suddenly from the sandy meadows, wheeling in great circles with a shining flutter of innumerable wings and shrill cries of surprise.

He traversed the fertile fields of Concabar, where the dust from the threshing-floors filled the air with a golden mist. At Baghistan, among the rich gardens watered by fountains from the rocky cliffs, he looked up at the mountain thrusting its immense rugged brow out over the sand and marvelled at the grandeur of the area he was traversing in his commitment to worshipping the prince of peace.

Over many a desolate pass, crawling painfully across the wind-swept shoulders of the dunes; down many a black mountain-gorge, where the river roared and raced before him like a savage guide; across many a smiling vale, with terraces of yellow limestone full of vines and fruit-trees; through various groves of trees and the dark towers of Zagros, walled in by precipices; into the ancient city of Chala, where the people of Samaria had been kept in captivity long ago; and out again by the mighty portal, riven through the encircling hills, where he saw the images of high priests sculptured on the walls of rocks with hands uplifted as if to bless the centuries of pilgrims; past the entrance of the narrow defile, filled from end to end with orchards of peaches and figs, through which the river Diyala foamed down to meet him; over the broad rice-fields, where the autumnal vapours spread their mists; following along the course of the river, under tremulous shadows of poplar and tamarind trees, among the lower hills; and out upon the flat plain, where the

The Legend of the Fourth Wise Man

road ran straight as an arrow through the stubble-fields and parched meadows; past the city of Ctesiphon, where the Parthian emperors reigned, and the vast metropolis of Seleucia, which Alexander built; across the swirling floods of the Tigris and the many channels of the Euphrates, flowing yellow through the vast cornfields, Artimus pressed onward until he arrived at nightfall of the tenth day of travel beneath the shattered walls of populous Babylon.

He knew that it was three hours' journey yet to the Temple of the Seven Spheres, and he must reach the place by midnight if he would find his comrades waiting. So he did not halt, but rode steadily across the stubble-fields.

A grove of date-palms made an island of gloom in the pale light brown sand of the desert that lay before him. As she passed into the shadows, Vasda slackened her pace, and began to pick her way more carefully forward in the quiet darkness.

Near the farther end of the darkness, an access of caution seemed to fall upon the determined camel as the two entered a grove. She scented some danger or difficulty. It was not in her heart to fly from it, only to be prepared for it, and to meet it wisely, as a good

The Legend of the Fourth Wise Man

camel should do. The grove was eerie and silent as the tomb; not a leaf rustled, not a bird sang.

Vasda felt her steps before her delicately, carrying her head low, and sighing now and then with apprehension. At last she gave a quick breath of anxiety and dismay, and stood stock-still, quivering in every muscle before a dark object in the shadow of the last palm-tree.

Artimus dismounted. The dim starlight revealed the form of a man lying across the road. His humble dress and the outline of his haggard face showed that he was probably one of the poor Hebrew exiles who still dwelt in great numbers in the vicinity. His pallid skin, dry and yellow as parchment, bore the mark of the deadly fever which ravaged the marsh-lands in autumn. The chill of death was in his lean hand, and, as Artimus lifted it, the arm fell limp and lifeless. He let go of it and it fell back inertly upon the motionless breast.

He looked away from the person with a thought of pity, consigning the body to that strange burial which the Magi deemed most fitting, the funeral of the desert from which the vultures rise on dark wings, and the beasts of prey slink furtively away, leaving only a heap of white bones in the sand to dry in the penetrating sun.

The Legend of the Fourth Wise Man

But, as he very reluctantly turned, a long, faint, ghostly, sombre sigh came from the man's lips. The brown, bony fingers closed convulsively on the hem of the Artimus' robe and held it fast.

Artimus' heart leaped to his throat, not with fear, but with intense resentment at the importunity of the blind delay. How could he stay here in the darkness to minister to a dying stranger? What claim had this unknown fragment of human life upon his compassion or his service? If he lingered but for an hour he could hardly reach Borsippa, where the other three Magi waited, at the appointed time. His companions would think he had given up the journey. They would go without him. He would lose his quest to see the new born king and lay offerings at his feet.

Yet, if he went on now, the man would surely die. If he stayed, life might be restored. His spirit throbbed and fluttered with the urgency of the crisis. Should he risk the great reward of his divine faith for the sake of a single deed of human love? Should he turn aside, if only for a moment, from the following of the star which shone so brightly overhead, to give a cup of cold water to a poor, perishing Hebrew? After all, was he not on his way to pay homage to another Hebrew?

J. Wayne Frye

The Legend of the Fourth Wise Man

"God of truth and purity," he prayed, "direct me in the holy path, the way of wisdom which thou only knowest."

Then he turned back to the sick man. Loosening the grasp of his hand, he carried him to a little mound at the foot of a palm-tree. He unbound the thick folds of the turban and opened the garment above the sunken breast. He brought water from one of the small canals near by and moistened the sufferer's brow and mouth. He mingled a mixture of one of those simple but potent remedies, which he carried always, as the Magi were physicians as well as astrologers. He poured it slowly between the colourless lips. Hour after hour he laboured as only a skilful healer of disease can do; and, at last, the man's strength returned until he was able to sit up and look about.

"Who art thou?" he said, in the rude dialect of the country, "and why hast thou sought me here to bring back my life?"

"I am Artimus, a Magi from the city of Ecbatana, and I am going to Jerusalem in search of one who is to be born King of the Jews, a great prince and deliverer for all men. I dare not delay any longer upon my journey, for the caravan that has waited for me may depart without me. It is most important to me to make

The Legend of the Fourth Wise Man

an offering to this glorious being who will be a deliverer of all mankind, a saviour who will shine a light of hope for all humanity. Here is all that I have left of my bread and wine. Here is a potion of the healing herbs which will cure you. When your strength is restored you can find the dwellings of the Hebrews among the houses of Babylon not much distance from here."

The Jew raised his trembling hands solemnly to heaven. "Now may the God of Abraham and Isaac and Jacob bless and prosper the journey of the merciful, and bring him in peace to his desired haven. But stay; I have nothing to give in return, only this that I can tell you where the Messiah must be sought. For our prophets have said that he should be born not in Jerusalem, but in Bethlehem of Judah. May the Lord bring you in safety to that place, because thou hast had pity upon the sick and broken. You have made a great sacrifice for your fellow man. "

Thanking the man for the attribution, Artimus quickly mounted his camel as it was already long past midnight. He did not see that one of the jewels has fell from his pocket. He rode in haste, and Vasda, restored by the brief rest, galloped eagerly through the silent plain and swam the channels of the river that had to be crossed. She put forth the remnant of her strength and fled over the ground like a gazelle.

J. Wayne Frye   35

The Legend of the Fourth Wise Man

The first beam of the sun sent Vasda's shadow before her as she entered upon the final phase of the journey, and the eyes of Artimus anxiously scanned the great mound of Nimrod and the Temple of the Seven Spheres, where he could discern no trace of his friends who had obviously tired of waiting for him and left, thinking they could tarry no longer.

The many-coloured terraces before them were shattered by the convulsions of nature, and crumbling under the repeated blows of human violence, still glittered like a ruined rainbow in the morning light, but his friends had apparently given up on him and departed in haste so as not to miss the coming birth of a great saviour.

Artimus rode swiftly around the hill of sand before him. He dismounted and climbed to the highest point, looking out towards the west, where he hoped to see the three Magi traversing the vast desert and few marshes before him.

The huge desolation of the marshes stretched away to the horizon and the border of the desert. Birds of prey stood by the stagnant pools and jackals skulked through the low bushes, but there was no sign of the caravan of wise men, far or near.

The Legend of the Fourth Wise Man

At the edge of the terrace he saw a little cairn of broken bricks, and under them a piece of parchment. He caught it up and read: "We have waited past the midnight and can delay no longer. We go to find the king. Follow us across the desert." Artimus sat down upon the ground and covered his head in despair.

"How can I cross the vast desert before me," he said to himself, "with no food and with a spent camel? I must return to Babylon, sell my sapphire, and buy a train of camels, and provision for the journey. I may never overtake my friends. Only God the merciful knows whether I shall not lose the sight of the king, because I tarried to show mercy."

At this point, the author feels it incumbent to mention that showing mercy, in essence, means acting with compassion and forgiveness, choosing not to inflict punishment or harm when one has the power to do so. It is about extending great kindness and understanding, particularly towards those who have wronged or hurt us, or who are in need. Mercy is a powerful force that can foster healing, reconciliation and positive change. This is something lacking in the world today, especially in the USA, where greed takes precedence over all other considerations. Just look at the cult of MAGA, where compassion is

The Legend of the Fourth Wise Man

considered a weakness, and where cruelty has been institutionalized as acceptable, especially when dealing with the poor, immigrants, downtrodden and non-whites. Yet these people, claiming to be Christians constantly invoke the name of Jesus, often to justify their cruelty. They forget that it was Jesus who said, "Blessed are the merciful, for they shall receive mercy" (Matthew 5:7). The Bible teaches that those people whom God has blessed the most abundantly should be merciful to other people. Joseph was merciful to his brothers after they sold him into slavery. David spared Saul's life after Saul tried to kill him. The story of the prodigal son is another example of repentance to receive mercy from God and its power to change you. In the parable, there were two sons. One son, the younger one, chose to go away from his father because of his own selfishness. He takes his inheritance to live as he pleases, while the older son faithfully stays with his father. When the younger son runs out of money, he realizes his foolishness and returns home expressing his great sorrow for his mistake. The father forgives him and celebrates his return. His repentance changed his heart and humbled him before God and his father. This shows that, when someone hurts you, you can forgive them and embrace them with great love. Mercy can be shown and someone's heart can change.

The Legend of the Fourth Wise Man

God delights in mercy, and a Christian should always show mercy. Mercy is giving money to the needy, food to the hungry or a bed to the homeless. "If there is among you a poor man of your brethren, within any of the gates in your land which the Lord your God is giving you, you shall not harden your heart nor shut your hand from your poor brother, but you shall open your hand wide to him and willingly lend him sufficient for his need, whatever he needs" (Deuteronomy 15:7-8). Showing mercy is not a fault. It is a virtue!

The Legend of the Fourth Wise Man

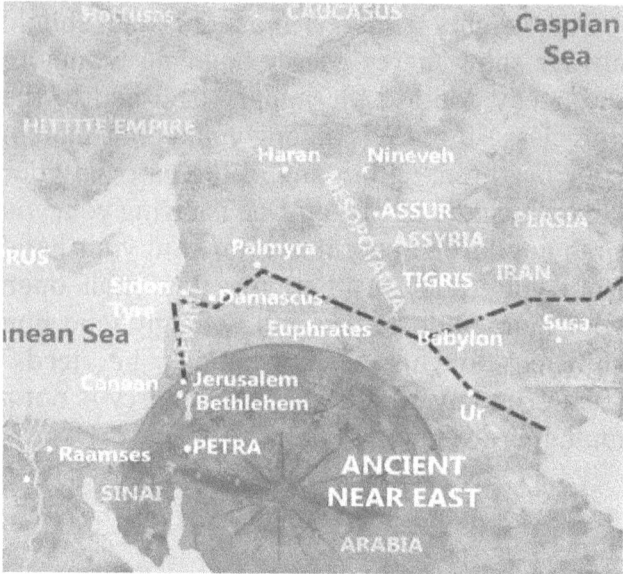

This ancient map, although grainy, is assumed to be accurate. The top broken lines are the route of the fourth wise man and the bottom broken lines the route of the three wise men.

The Legend of the Fourth Wise Man

Chapter 3
Give Thee Peace

*To purchase three precious jewels he sold
everything
To have valuable gifts to give to the new born
king.
Missing his rendezvous with the three other
Magi,
He journeyed across a cruel desert under
a starry sky.*

There was a silence as Artimus journeyed ever onward in what might be called the Hall of Dreams, where he was contemplating where the other wise men might be on the same route that lay ahead of him. And through this silence he saw, but very dimly, his figure passing over the dreary undulations of the desert, high upon the back of his camel, rocking steadily onward like a ship over the waves.

The land of death spread its cruel net around him. The stony wastes bore no fruit but briers and thorns. The dark ledges of rock thrust themselves above the surface here and there, like the bones of perished monsters. Arid and inhospitable mountain ranges rose before him, furrowed with dry channels of ancient torrents, white and ghastly as scars on the face of nature. Shifting hills of treacherous sand were heaped like tombs along the horizon. By day, the fierce heat pressed its intolerable burden on the quivering air; and no living creature moved on the swooning earth, except tiny insects scuttling through the parched bushes or lizards vanishing in the clefts of the rocks. By night the jackals prowled and barked in the distance, and a lion made the black ravines echo with its hollow roaring, while a bitter, blighting chill followed the fever of the day. Through heat and cold, the Magi moved steadily onward.

Then he saw the gardens and orchards of Damascus, watered by the flowing streams with their sloping swards inlaid with bloom, and their thickets of myrrh and roses. He saw the

The Legend of the Fourth Wise Man

long, snowy ridge of Mount Hermon, the dark groves of cedars, the valley of the Jordan River, the blue waters of Lake Galilee, the fertile plain of Esdraelon, the hills of Ephraim and the highlands of Judah. Through all these the figure of Artimus moved steadily onward, until he arrived at Bethlehem. And it was the third day after the three wise men had come to that place and had found Mary and Joseph with the young child, Jesus, and had laid their gifts of gold, frankincense and myrrh at his feet.

Then, Artimus drew near, weary, but full of hope, bearing his ruby and his pearl to offer to the king. "For now at last," he said, "I shall surely find him, though it be alone, and later than my brethren. This is the place of which the Hebrew exile told me that the prophets had spoken, and here I shall behold the rising of the great light. But I must inquire about the visit of my brethren, and to what house the star directed them, and to whom they presented their tribute."

The streets of the village seemed to be deserted, and Artimus wondered whether the men had all gone up to the hill-pastures to bring down their sheep. From the open door of a low stone cottage he heard the sound of a woman's voice singing softly. He entered and found a young mother hushing her baby to rest.

The Legend of the Fourth Wise Man

She told him of the strangers from the Far East who had appeared in the village three days before, and how they said that a star had guided them to the place where Joseph of Nazareth was lodging with his dear wife and new-born child, and how they had paid reverence to the child and given him many rich gifts.

"The travellers disappeared again," she continued, "as suddenly as they had come. We were afraid at the strangeness of their visit. We could not understand it. The man of Nazareth took the babe and his mother and fled away that same night secretly, and it was whispered that they were going far away to Egypt. Ever since, there has been a spell upon the village; something evil hanging over it. They say that the Roman soldiers are coming from the city of Jerusalem to force a new tax from us, and the men have driven the flocks and herds far back among the hills and hidden themselves to escape it."

Artimus listened to her gentle, timid speech, and the child in her arms looked up in his face and smiled, stretching out its rosy hands to touch him. His heart warmed to the gentle touch. It seemed like a greeting of love and trust to one who had journeyed long in loneliness and perplexity, fighting with his own

The Legend of the Fourth Wise Man

doubts and fears, and following a light that was veiled in clouds now with its brightness fading.

"Might not this child have been the promised prince?" he asked within himself, as he touched its soft cheek. "Kings have been born ere now in lowlier houses than this, and the favourite of the stars may rise even from a cottage. But it has not seemed good to the God of wisdom to reward my search so soon and so easily. The one whom I seek has gone before me, and now I must follow the new king to Egypt."

The young mother laid the babe in its cradle, and rose to minister to the wants of the strange guest that fate had brought into her house. She set food before him for it is generally the poor, rather than the rich, who extend the helpful hand to those in need. It was the plain fare of peasants, but willingly offered, and therefore full of refreshment for the soul as well as for the body. Artimus accepted it gratefully; and, as he ate, the child fell into a happy slumber, and murmured sweetly in its dreams and a great peace filled the quiet room.

Suddenly there came the pounding noise of a wild confusion and great, screaming, turbulent uproar in the streets of the village, a shrieking and wailing of women's voices, a clangour of brazen trumpets and a tremendous clashing of

The Legend of the Fourth Wise Man

swords and a wild desperate cry: "The soldiers! The soldiers of Herod! They are killing our children."

The young mother's face grew white with terror. She clasped her child to her bosom, and crouched motionless in the darkest corner of the room, covering him with the folds of her robe, lest he should wake and cry.

But Artimus went quickly and stood in the doorway of the house. His broad shoulders filled the portal from side to side, and the peak of his cap all but touched the top sill, as the evil of the oligarchic rulers preyed unabated on the poor innocents just as they do in today's world, where those in power rule with impunity in a world where the downtrodden are crushed under the yoke of the mighty.

The cruel soldiers came hurrying down the street with bloody hands and dripping swords. At the sight of the stranger in his imposing dress they hesitated with surprise. The captain of the band approached the threshold to thrust him aside. But Artimus did not stir. His face was as calm as though he were watching the stars, and in his eyes there burned that steady radiance before which even the mighty lion shrinks and the fierce hound pauses in his leap. He held the soldier silently for an instant, and then said in a low voice: "There is no one in this place but me, and I am waiting to give this jewel to the prudent captain who will leave me in peace."

He showed the ruby he had intended for Jesus, glistening in the hollow of his hand like a great drop of royal blood. The captain was amazed at the splendour of the gem. The pupils of his eyes expanded with desire, and the hard lines of greed wrinkled around his lips. He stretched out his hand and took the ruby as he said to his men, "March on! There is no child here."

The clamour and the clang of arms passed wildly down the blood stained street as the headlong fury of the chase swept by the secret adobe where the trembling mother and child were hidden. Artimus re-entered the cottage, closing the door. He turned his face to the east and whispered, "God of truth, forgive my sin! I have said the thing that is not true to save the life of a child. And my great gift is gone. I have spent for man that which was meant for God. Shall I ever be worthy to see the face of the king?"

But the voice of the frantic woman, weeping for joy in the shadow behind him, said very gently as tears streamed down her cheeks,

The Legend of the Fourth Wise Man

"Because thou hast saved the life of my little one, may the Lord bless thee and keep thee; the Lord make His face to shine upon thee and be gracious unto thee; the Lord lift up His countenance upon thee and give thee peace."

Woodprint of Lodovico Mazzolino's
The Infanticide in Bethlehem

J. Wayne Frye

Chapter 4
The Place Called Golgotha

Where he went in Judea, he looked for the new
born king,
But his search became a frustrating
futile thing,
Bringing a deep sense of inner sorrow
to his mind.
Throughout the country, the new born king he
could not find.

Then again there was a silence in the Night of
Dreams, deeper and more mysterious than the
first interval. The times of Artimus were
flowing very swiftly under the stillness of that

The Legend of the Fourth Wise Man

clinging fog that now seemed to hang over each step in his journey, as he tried to locate the king which seemed to keep eluding him. He caught only a glimpse, here and there, of hope shining through the shadows that concealed the course taken by the baby and his beloved mother and earthly father.

He moved among the throngs of men in populous Egypt, seeking everywhere for traces of the household that had come down from Bethlehem, and finding them under the spreading sycamore-trees of Heliopolis, and beneath the walls of the Roman fortress of New Babylon beside the Nile, traces so faint and dim that they vanished before him continually, as footprints on the hard river sand glistened for a moment with moisture and then disappeared.

He thought he was hot on the trail at the foot of the pyramids, which lifted their sharp points into the intense saffron glow of the sunset sky, changeless monuments of the perishable glory and the imperishable hope of man. He looked up into the vast countenance of the crouching Sphinx and vainly tried to read the meaning of her calm eyes and smiling mouth. Was it, indeed, the mockery of all effort and all aspiration, as Tigranes had said the cruel jest of a riddle that had no answer, a search that never can succeed? Or was there a touch of pity and

The Legend of the Fourth Wise Man

encouragement in that inscrutable smile, a promise that even the defeated should attain a victory, and the disappointed should discover a prize, and the ignorant could be made wise, and the blind could see and the wandering might come upon their quest at last?

He got word of this remarkable child as the years went by, having just missed him in an obscure house of Alexandria, taking counsel with a Hebrew rabbi who had seen the boy, mother and father. The venerable man, bending over the rolls of parchment on which the prophecies of Israel were written, read aloud the prophetic words which foretold the sufferings of the promised Messiah, the despising and rejection of men, the coming of sorrows for Him and the acquaintance of great grief.

"And remember, my son," said the rabbi, fixing his deep-set eyes upon the face of Artimus, "the King whom you are seeking is not to be found in a palace, nor among the rich and powerful. If the light of the world and the glory of Israel had been appointed to come with the greatness of earthly splendour, it must have appeared long ago. For no son of Abraham will ever again rival the power which Joseph had in the palaces of Egypt, or the magnificence of Solomon throned between the lions in

The Legend of the Fourth Wise Man

Jerusalem. But the light for which the world is waiting is a new light, the glory that shall rise out of patient and triumphant suffering. And the kingdom which is to be established forever is a new kingdom, the royalty of perfect and unconquerable love. I do not know how this shall come to pass, nor how the turbulent kings and peoples of earth shall be brought to acknowledge the Messiah and pay homage to him. But this I know. Those who seek Him will do well to look among the poor and the lowly, the sorrowful and the oppressed, for he sees the wealthy and exalted as pariahs and the poor as truly worthy of the kingdom of God."

So he never saw the other wise men again, because he never returned home in all those years, travelling as he was from place to place still searching for the one he had just missed. In his searching among the people, he would often just miss Him, but hear tales of the boy's grandeur from those with whom the little family from Bethlehem found a refuge. He passed through countries where famine lay heavy upon the land, and the poor were crying for bread. He made his dwelling in plague-stricken cities, where the sick were languishing in the bitter companionship of helpless misery. He visited the oppressed and the afflicted in the gloom of subterranean prisons, the crowded wretchedness of slave-markets and the weary

The Legend of the Fourth Wise Man

toil of galley-ships. In all this populous and intricate world of anguish, though he found none to worship, he found many to help. He fed the hungry, clothed the naked, healed the sick and comforted the captive; and his years went by more swiftly than the weaver's shuttle that flashes back and forth through the loom while the web grows and the invisible pattern is completed.

It seemed almost as if he had forgotten his quest. But once he saw what he thought might have been Jesus for a moment as he stood alone at sunrise, waiting outside the temple in Jerusalem. He had taken from a secret resting-place in his bosom the pearl, the last of his jewels. As he looked at it, a mellower lustre, a soft and iridescent light, full of shifting gleams of azure and rose, trembled upon its surface. It seemed to have absorbed some reflection of the colours of the lost sapphire and ruby. So the profound, secret purpose of a noble life draws into itself the memories of past joy and past sorrow. All that has helped it, all that has hindered it is transfused by a subtle magic into its very essence. It becomes more luminous and precious the longer it is carried close to the warmth of the beating and pure heart. Then, at last, while he was thinking of this pearl, and of its meaning, he approached the end of the story that had captivated him for so long.

The Legend of the Fourth Wise Man

Three-and-thirty years of the life of Artimus had passed away, and he was still a pilgrim and a seeker after light. His hair, once darker than cliffs of coal, was now white as the wintry snow that covered those mountains of coal. His eyes that once flashed like flames of fire were dull as embers smouldering among the ashes.

Worn and weary and ready to die, but still looking for the king, he had come for the last time to Jerusalem. He had often visited the holy city before, and had searched through all its lanes and crowded hovels and black prisons without finding any trace of the family of Nazarenes who had fled from Bethlehem long ago. But now it seemed as if he must make one more effort, and something whispered in his heart that, at last, he might succeed. It was the season of the Passover. The city was thronged with strangers. The children of Israel, scattered in far lands all over the world, had returned to the temple for the great feast, and there had been a confusion of various tongues in the narrow streets for many days.

But on this day there was a singular agitation visible in the multitude. The sky was veiled with a portentous gloom, and currents of excitement seemed to flash through the crowd like the thrill which shakes the forest on the eve of a storm. A secret tide was sweeping them all

The Legend of the Fourth Wise Man

one way. The clatter of sandals, and the soft, thick sound of thousands of bare feet shuffling over the stones, flowed unceasingly along the street that led to the main city gate.

Artimus joined company with a group of people from his own country, Parthian Jews, who had come up to keep the Passover, and inquired of them the cause of the tumult, and where all the people were going.

"We are going," they answered, "to the place called Golgotha, outside the city walls, where there is to be an execution. Have you not heard what has happened? Two famous robbers are to be crucified, and with them another, called Jesus of Nazareth, a man who has done many wonderful works among the people, so that they love him greatly. But the priests and elders have said that he must die, because he gave himself out to be the Son of God, and Pilate has sent him to the cross, because he said that he was the 'King of the Jews.'"

How strangely these familiar words fell upon the tired heart of Artimus! They had led him for a lifetime over land and sea. And now they came to him darkly and mysteriously like a message of despair. The King of Jews had come, but he had been denied and cast out. He was about to perish. Perhaps he was already dying.

The Legend of the Fourth Wise Man

Could it be the same who had been born in Bethlehem thirty-three years ago at whose birth the star had appeared in heaven, and of whose coming the prophets had spoken?

Artimus' heart beat unsteadily with that troubled, doubtful apprehension which is the norm of old age. But he said within himself, "The ways of God are stranger than the thoughts of men, and it may be that I shall find the king, at last, in the hands of His enemies, and shall come in time to offer my pearl for His ransom before He dies."

So the old man followed the multitude with slow and painful steps towards the main gate of the city. Just beyond the entrance of the guard-house, a troop of Macedonian soldiers came down the street, dragging a young girl with torn dress and dishevelled hair. As Artimus paused to look at her with compassion, she broke suddenly from the hands of her tormentors, and threw herself at his feet, clasping him around the knees. She had seen his white cap and the winged circle on his breast, the sign he was a Magi and might offer her some help.

"Have pity on me," she cried, "and save me, for the sake of the God! I also am a daughter of the true religion, which is taught by the Magi.

The Legend of the Fourth Wise Man

My father was a merchant, but he has died, and I am seized for his debts to be sold as a slave. Save me from worse than death!"

Artimus trembled. It was the old conflict in his soul, which had come to him in the palm-grove of Babylon and in the cottage at Bethlehem, the eternal conflict between the expectation of faith and the impulse of love for fellow humans who are suffering. Twice the gift which he had consecrated to the worship of religion had been drawn from his hand to the service of humanity. This was the third trial, the ultimate probation, the final and irrevocable choice. This was the last gift he had, a gift that might save Jesus from death.

Was it his great opportunity, or his last temptation? He could not tell. One thing only was clear in the darkness of his mind. It was inevitable. And does not the inevitable come from God?

One thing only was sure to his divided heart, to rescue this helpless girl would be a true deed of love. And is not love the light of the soul?

He took the pearl from his gown. Never had it seemed so luminous, so radiant, so full of tender, living lustre. He laid it in the hand of the slave.

The Legend of the Fourth Wise Man

"This is your ransom, daughter! It is the last of my treasures which I kept for the king."

While he spoke, the penetratingly heavy darkness of the sky thickened, and shuddering tremors ran through the earth, heaving convulsively like the breast of one who struggles with mighty grief.

The walls of the houses rocked to and fro. Stones were loosened and crashed into the street. Dust clouds filled the air. The soldiers fled in terror, reeling like drunken men. But Artimus and the girl whom he had ransomed crouched helpless beneath the walls which surrounded them.

What had he to fear? What had he to live for? He had given away the last remnant of his tribute for the king. He had parted with the last hope of finding Him. The quest was over, and it had failed. But, even in that thought, accepted and embraced, there was peace. It was not resignation. It was not submission. It was something more profound and searching. He knew that all was well, because he had done the best that he could, from day to day. He had been true to the light that had been given to him. He had looked for more. And if he had not found it. If a failure was all that came out of his life, doubtless that was the best that was possible. He had not seen the revelation of "life everlasting, incorruptible and immortal."

One more lingering pulsation of the now recognizable rumblings of an earthquake quivered through the ground. A heavy tile, shaken from the roof, fell and struck him on the temple. He lay breathless and pale, with his grey head resting on the young girl's shoulder, and the blood trickling from the wound. As she bent over him, fearing that he was dead, there came a voice through the twilight, very small and still, like music sounding from a distance, in which the notes are clear but the words are lost. The girl turned to see if someone had spoken from the window above them, but she saw no one.

Then Artimus' lips began to move as he whispered to the air about him: "When I saw the hungry did I not feed them? When I saw the thirsty did I not give them drink? When saw I a strange did I not extend the hand of friendship? When I saw the naked did I not buy them some clothes? When saw I the sick or those in prison, did I not extend the hand of sympathy? Three-and-thirty years have I looked for you; but I have never seen your face."

He ceased, and a sweet voice came. And the woman heard it also very faintly and far away.

The Legend of the Fourth Wise Man

But now it seemed as though she understood the words: "*Verily I say unto thee, inasmuch as thou hast done it unto one of the least of these my brethren, thou hast done it unto me.*"

A calm radiance of wonder and joy lit the pale face of Artimus like the first ray of dawn on a snowy mountain-peak. One long breath of relief exhaled gently from his lips, as he struggled to his feet, touched the lady he had saved and said, "Now that you have procured your freedom with my pearl, I have no gift for the King of the Jews. I go now to see the death of He whom I have sought for so long. I can feel my own death coming, but I must lay eyes on Him whom I have sought for so long before I die. Can you, my dear, help an old man to the place called Golgotha? "

The Legend of the Fourth Wise Man

Chapter 5
Stare in Wonderment and Awe

*In passing years he spent his jewels helping
others in need.
Compassionately, he gave of himself
in word and deed.
His jewels were gone; he was empty,
lost and forlorn.
He had nothing to give to Him that
as a king was born.*

Artimus, along the way, slowly moving toward Golgotha, stopped to rest on some steps where a man sat crying. "Why do you weep," asked Artimus. as he took a seat beside him.

The Legend of the Fourth Wise Man

"I weep for the man I watched being scourged by the Roman soldiers before being taken up to the Place of the Skulls, also called Golgotha, a man who has done no wrong. I see today because of that man. I was blind, and he touched my eyes and gave me sight. He is truly the son of God."

"Tell me," said Artimus. "Tell me all you know of this wondrous man."

"I can relate it all, because His gospel was related to me by several of his disciples. The beginning of the gospel of Jesus Christ, as it is written by the prophets said simply that God would send a messenger to prepare the way before His arrival, and that it would be the voice of one crying in the wilderness. That was John the Baptist who preached the baptism of repentance for the remission of sins. And there went out unto him all the land of Judaea, and they of Jerusalem, and they were all baptized of him in the river of Jordan, confessing their sins. And John was clothed with camel's hair and with a girdle of a skin about his loins, and he ate locusts and wild honey and preached that there cometh one mightier than him, the latchet of whose shoes John was not worthy to stoop down and unloose. He indeed baptized people with water: but he said that the one coming would baptize with the Holy Ghost."

The Legend of the Fourth Wise Man

Artimus and his companion, the good woman, Rachael, were enthralled by the man's renditions about Jesus.

He leaned forward and said, "And it came to pass in those days, that Jesus came from Nazareth of Galilee and was baptized of John in the Jordan. And straightway coming up out of the water, he saw the heavens opened, and the Spirit like a dove descending upon him, and there came a voice from heaven, saying that Jesus was my beloved son in whom I am pleased."

"And immediately the spirit forced Jesus into the wilderness. And he was there in the wilderness forty days, tempted of Satan; and was with the wild beasts, and the angels ministered unto him. Now after that John was put in prison, Jesus came into Galilee, preaching the gospel of the kingdom of God, encouraging people to know that the kingdom of God was at hand and that all should repent and believe wholeheartedly in the gospel."

The man told them of how as Jesus walked by the Sea of Galilee, he saw Simon and Andrew his brother casting a net into the sea: for they were fishers. And Jesus said unto them that they should follow Him, become fishers of men and spread the gospel."

J. Wayne Frye 63

The Legend of the Fourth Wise Man

Straightway they forsook their nets and followed Jesus. And when he had gone a little farther, he saw James, the son of Zebedee, and John his brother, who also were in the ship mending their nets. And straightway he called them, and they left their father Zebedee in the ship with the hired servants and went after Jesus. And he continued his tale as Rachael and Artimus were enthralled with every single word.

He told them how they all, following Jesus, went into Capernaum, and on the Sabbath day Jesus entered into the synagogue and taught. And he told them of how all there were astonished at his doctrine, for he taught them as one that had authority. And there was in their synagogue a man with an unclean spirit; and he cried out to be left alone, accusing Jesus of coming to destroy them as the holy one of God, but Jesus commanded the unclean spirit to leave him and the bad spirit immediately left the man. All there were amazed, insomuch that they questioned among themselves the power exhibited by this man. Immediately, his fame spread abroad throughout the entire region around about Galilee.

Warming to his story he said, "When they came out of the synagogue, they entered into the house of Simon and Andrew, with James and John. But Simon's wife's mother lay sick of a fever. Jesus came and took her by the hand and lifted her up and immediately the fever left her. Thus was the coveted power of Jesus. And when the sun set, the people brought unto Him all that were diseased and thoser that were possessed with devils. Throngs from the city gathered together at the door. He healed many that were sick of various diseases, and cast out many demons and suffered not the devils to speak, because they knew Him and feared Him. In the morning, rising up a great while before day, he went out and departed into a solitary place and there prayed. And Simon and they that were with him followed after Him. And when they had found Jesus, they said unto Him that all men sought His blessing."

"He said to them that they should go into nearby towns so that He may preach there also, and he preached in their synagogues throughout all Galilee, and cast out devils and cured the ill. And there came a leper to Him, beseeching Him, and kneeling down to Him, and asking Him to make him clean. Jesus, moved with compassion, put forth his hand, and touched him, and said for him to be clean, and immediately the leprosy departed from him, and he was cleansed. And He told the man to go forth and tell the priests what had happened, which he did, and it was this

The Legend of the Fourth Wise Man

approbation which would start the trouble, the trouble which would be compounded as word blazed abroad the land about Jesus and His healing power. Soon, He could no longer openly enter into any city or seek solace in the desert without people finding Him in every quarter and asking for blessings.

So spellbound by the tale from the formerly blind man who had been healed by Jesus were the two that they followed every word as if they were in a state of rapture. The tale continued as the two sat spellbound.

Jesus entered into Capernaum after some days; and it was noticed by all there when He went into a house. Straightway, many were gathered at the house insomuch that there was no room to receive them, He stood in the doorway and preached the word for what seemed like hours. And they came unto Him, bringing one sick of the palsy, many with other afflictions, until they could not come unto Him for the pressing of humanity. Still, He patiently allowed all to come and be healed, not turning away a single person. When Jesus saw their faith, He was overwhelmed with love for them all.

But there were certain of the scribes (an ancient Jewish record-keeper) who came there, and reasoning in their hearts that this man was speaking such blasphemies, as only God could heal and forgive sins. Immediately when Jesus perceived in his spirit that they so reasoned within themselves, he asked them why they should reason these things in their hearts, asking them whether it was easier to say to the sick of the palsy that their sins be forgiven or to tell them to arise and take up their beds and walk? He told them all that they may know that the Son-of-Man had the power on earth to forgive sins and to heal the sick.

He went forth again by the sea side; and all the multitude resorted unto Him, and He taught them. And as He passed by, he saw Levi the son of Alphaeus sitting at the receipt of custom, and said unto him, "follow me." And he arose and followed him.

It came to pass that, as Jesus sat at in Levi's house, many publicans and sinners sat also together with Jesus and his disciples for there were many that followed Him. And when the scribes and Pharisees saw Him eat with publicans and sinners, they said unto his disciples, "How is it that he eats and drinks with publicans and sinners?"

When Jesus heard it, He said unto them with great conviction; "They that are whole have no need of the physician, but they that are sick I came not to call the righteous, but sinners to repentance."

And the disciples of John and of the Pharisees used to fasting came and said unto Him, "Why do the disciples of John and of the Pharisees fast, but your disciples fast not?"

Jesus said unto them, again with great conviction, "Can the children of the bride chamber fast, while the bridegroom is with them? As long as they have the bridegroom with them, they cannot fast. But the days will come when the bridegroom shall be taken away from them, and then shall they fast in those days. No man also seweth a piece of new cloth on an old garment else the new piece that filled it up taketh away from the old, and the rent is made worse. And no man putteth new wine into old bottles, else the new wine doth burst the bottles, and the wine is spilled, and the bottles will be marred but new wine must be put into new bottles."

And it came to pass, that He went through the corn fields on the Sabbath day; and His disciples, as they went, plucked the ears of corn. And the Pharisees said unto Him, "Behold, why do they on the Sabbath day that which is not lawful?"

The Legend of the Fourth Wise Man

And Jesus said unto them, "Have ye never read what David did, when he had need and was hungered? He and they that were with him? How he went into the house of God in the days of Abiathar, the high priest, and did eat the showbread(twelve loaves placed every Sabbath in the Jewish Temple and eaten by the priests at the end of the week), which is not lawful to eat but for the priests, and gave also to them which were with him? The Sabbath was made for man, and not man for the Sabbath; therefore, the Son of Man is Lord also of the Sabbath."

Artimus and Rachael, whom he had saved, as he had saved many others over the years, were so enthralled by the man's tales of Jesus that they could not speak, but only stare in wonderment and awe.

Woodcut of Jesus teaching. Athenian Illustrated Bible (Printed 1552).

The Legend of the Fourth Wise Man

Ancient woodcut of Jesus in a house teaching.

The Legend of the Fourth Wise Man

Chapter 6
They Did So and Were Made Whole

Now an old man, Artimus came
to Jerusalem again.
On his face and in his heart were
emptiness and pain.
All his life had been a failure,
looking for the king.
Hopelessness was the only song
his heart could sing.

The man's tale continued as he told of when Jesus entered into the synagogue on a Sabbath, and there was a man there who had a withered hand. And the priests watched Him, whether He would heal him on the Sabbath day; that they might accuse Him.

And Jesus, to the man who had the withered hand said, "Stand forth." He then turned to the priests and said, "Is it lawful to do good on the Sabbath or to do evil? To save life or to kill?"

All the priests stood in silence, not uttering a response. When Jesus had looked around at each of them with anger, being grieved for the hardness of their hearts, He said unto the afflicted man, "Stretch forth thine hand."

He stretched it out and his hand was restored whole as the other. And the Pharisees went forth, and straightway took secret counsel with the dreaded Herodians against Jesus, discussing how they might conspire to destroy Him. This was par for the Herodians, as they were a political faction in ancient Judea, much like the accursed and vile MAGA movement in the USA today that had no sympathy for the poor and downtrodden, and were hypocritical in their approach to all things holy. They played at being religious, but in their hearts were an affront to the love and kindness displayed by Jesus. Like the Trump acolytes today, they were a group of people who favored the rule of the elite and the subservience of those they considered inferior.

The Legend of the Fourth Wise Man

Before any action could be taken against Him, Jesus withdrew with his disciples to the sea, and a great multitude from Galilee followed Him, and from Judaea, and from Jerusalem, and from Idumaea and from beyond Jordan. About Tyre and Sidon, a great multitude, when they had heard what great things He did, came unto Him. And he spoke to his disciples that a small ship should wait on Him because of the multitude, lest they should overwhelm Him. For He had healed many; insomuch that they pressed forward to touch Him, as many had plagues of various types and were possessed by unclean spirits.

When they saw Him, all fell down before Him, and cried, "Thou art the Son of God."

He healed many and charged them that they should not make him known to the authorities. He went into a mountain, and called unto his original followers to come with Him. And he ordained twelve, that they should be with him, and that he might send them forth to preach, and to have power to heal sicknesses, and to cast out devils. And Simon, he surnamed Peter; and James the son of Zebedee and John the brother of James, and he surnamed them Boanerges, which is the sons of thunder. He called upon Andrew, Philip, Bartholomew, Matthew, Thomas, James, Thaddaeus, Simon the Canaanite, and Judas Iscariot, who would become His eventual betrayer.

After a time, they hungered and went into a house. Alas, the multitudes, getting word of where He was, came together again, so that they could not so much as eat bread as the crush of people was so great.

The priests got word of Him, and they came down from Jerusalem as they said He was a servant of Beelzebub and by the prince of the devils cast out devils. This was an evil man, according to them, a man who was not obeying the laws properly.

Meanwhile, Jesus was spellbinding crowds with his parables. He said when he heard of being accused of serving Satan, "How can Satan cast out Satan. And if a kingdom be divided against itself that kingdom cannot stand. And if a house be divided against itself that house cannot stand. And if Satan rise up against himself and be divided, he cannot stand, but hath an end. No man can enter into a strong man's house and spoil his goods, except he will first bind the strong man, and then he will spoil his house. Verily I say unto you all sins shall be forgiven unto the sons of men, and blasphemies wherewith so ever they shall blaspheme, but he that shall blaspheme against the Holy Ghost.

The Legend of the Fourth Wise Man

There came then his brethren and his mother, and, standing without, sent unto Him, calling Him. And the multitude sat about Him, and they said unto Him, "Behold, thy mother and thy brethren without seek for thee."

He answered them, saying, "Who is my mother or my brethren?" He looked around at those who sat about him, and said, "Behold my mother and my brethren! For whosoever shall do the will of God is the same as my brother, my sister and my mother."

It was not long after that when he arose and left to begin again to teach by the seaside, and there was gathered unto him a great multitude, so that he entered into a ship, and sat in the sea, and the whole multitude was by the sea on the land. And he taught them many things by parables, and said unto them in His doctrine, "Hearken; behold, there went out a sower to sow, and it came to pass, as he sowed, some fell by the way side, and the fowls of the air came and devoured it up. And some fell on stony ground, where it had not much earth; and immediately it sprang up, because it had no depth of earth: but when the sun was up it was scorched, and because it had no root it withered away. And some fell among thorns, and the thorns grew up and choked it, and it yielded no fruit. And other fell on good ground and did yield fruit that sprang up."

The Legend of the Fourth Wise Man

And when he was alone, they that were about Him with the twelve asked of Him the parable. And He said unto them, "Unto you it is given to know the mystery of the kingdom of God, but unto them that are without, all these things are done in parables that seeing they may see, and not perceive; and hearing they may hear, and not understand lest at any time they should be converted and their sins should be forgiven them. Know ye not this parable? And how then will ye know all parables? The sower soweth the word. And these are they by the way side, where the word is sown, but when they have heard, Satan cometh immediately and taketh away the word that was sown in their hearts. And these are they likewise which are sown on stony ground; who, when they have heard the word, immediately receive it with gladness and have no root in themselves, and so endure but for a time. Afterward, when affliction or persecution ariseth for the word's sake, immediately they are offended. And these are they which are sown among thorns; such as hear the word, and the cares of this world and the deceitfulness of riches, and the lusts of other things entering in choke the word and it becometh unfruitful. And these are they which are sown on good ground, such as hear the word and receive it, and bring forth fruit and understand that man is a creature of and for God."

The Legend of the Fourth Wise Man

According to the teller to whom Artimus was intently listening, as was his companion, Jesus continued his explanation. "Is a candle brought to be put under a bushel, or under a bed and not to be set on a candlestick? For there is nothing hidden, which shall not be manifested; neither was anything kept secret, but that it should come abroad. If any men have ears to hear, let him hear. Take heed what ye hear with what measure ye mete, it shall be measured to you; and unto you that hear shall more be given. For he that hath to him shall be given: and he that hath not, from him shall be taken even that which he hath. So is the kingdom of God, as if a man should cast seed into the ground; and should sleep, and rise night and day, and the seed should spring and grow up, he knoweth not how. For the earth bringeth forth fruit of herself; first the blade, then the ear, after that the full corn in the ear. But when the fruit is brought forth, immediately he putteth in the sickle, because the harvest is come. Whereunto shall we liken the kingdom of God? With what comparison shall we compare it? It is like a grain of mustard seed, which, when it is sown in the earth is less than all the seeds that be in the earth, but when it is sown it groweth up and becometh greater than all herbs, and shooteth out great branches so that the fowls of the air may lodge under the shadow of it."

The Legend of the Fourth Wise Man

And with many such parables spake He the word unto them, as they were able to hear it. But without a parable spake He not unto them, and when they were alone, He expounded all things to his disciples. And the same day, when the evening was come, He said unto them from the ship which they were on "Let us pass over unto the other side."

And when they had gone from the vast multitude of people, there were also with Him other little ships, and there arose a great storm of wind, and the waves furiously beat into the ship. He was in the hinder part of the ship, asleep on a pillow; and they awakened Him, and said unto him, "Master, carest thou not that we perish?"

He arose, and rebuked the wind, and said unto the sea, "Peace, be still."

At that very instance the wind ceased, and there was a great calm as he said unto them, "Why are ye so fearful? How is it that ye have no faith?"

He then lifted his head with great reverence on his face toward the heavens and said of himself with great conviction, "What manner of man is this, that even the wind and the sea obey Him?"

J. Wayne Frye

The Legend of the Fourth Wise Man

Woodprint from 1777: Jesus Calming the Storm

J. Wayne Frye

The Legend of the Fourth Wise Man

They came over unto the other side of the sea, into the country of the Gadarenes, and when He came out of the ship, immediately there met Him out of the tombs a man with an unclean spirit, who had his dwelling among the tombs; and no man could bind him, no, not with chains, because that he had been often bound with chains and restraints, and the chains had been plucked asunder by him and the restraints broken in pieces. No man could tame him. And always, night and day, he was in the mountains, and in the tombs, crying and cutting himself with stones. Yet, when he saw Jesus afar off, he ran and worshipped him, and cried with a loud voice, saying, "What have I to do with thee, Jesus, thou Son of the highest God? I adjure thee by God that thou torment me not."

Jesus said unto him: "Come out of the man, thou unclean spirit," And he asked him: "What is thy name?" And the man possessed answered, "My name is Legion: for we are many."

The man pleaded with Jesus to free him of all the demons possessing him. Jesus looked high on the mountain above and saw a great herd of swine feeding. Forthwith, Jesus bade the spirits to leave the man. And the unclean spirits went out, and entered into the swine, and the herd ran violently down a steep place into the sea, and were choked in the sea. And they that fed the swine fled, and told it in the city and in the country. And they went out to see what it was that was done. And they came to Jesus to see him that was possessed with the devil, and had the legion of spirits within before, sitting and clothed, and in his right mind and they were afraid. They that saw it told of how it befell to him that was previously possessed with the devil and also concerning the swine. And they became afraid, fearful of the power within Jesus.

In their presence, Jesus turned to the man now freed of spirits and told him to go home to his friends and family to tell them of the great things the Lord had done for him, and how compassion from the Lord triumphed."

He departed, and began to proclaim in the city of Decapolis the great things Jesus had done for him, and all people there did marvel.

When Jesus was passed over again by ship unto the other side of the sea, many people gathered unto him when he sat foot on land, and he was deep upon that land. Then, there came one of the rulers of the synagogue, Jairus by name; and when he saw Jesus he instinctively fell at his feet, and besought him greatly, saying, "My little daughter lies at the point of death: I pray thee, come and lay thy hands on her that she may be healed and she shall live."

And Jesus went with Him; and many people followed Jesus and thronged Him. A certain woman, who had an issue with pain for twelve years and had suffered many things from many physicians, and had spent all that she had in search of cures, but only grew worse came up behind Jesus and touched his garment, saying, "If I may touch but His clothes, I shall be whole again."

Straightway she felt her body was miraculously healed of that plague. And Jesus, immediately knowing in himself that virtue had gone out of Him, turned about and said, "Who touched my clothes?"

His disciples said unto Him, "Thou seest the multitude thronging thee, and sayest thou who touched me?"

He looked around to see she who had touched His garment, but the woman, fearing and trembling, knowing what was done in her, came and fell down before Him, and told Him all the truth of the healing. He said, "Daughter, thy faith hath made thee whole; go in peace, and be free of thy plague."

The Legend of the Fourth Wise Man

While he yet spoke, there came from Jairus' house word that his daughter had died. Jairus bowed his head and sobbed. Jesus touched his shoulder and said, "Be not afraid, only believe."

No one followed Jesus, save Peter, James and John, the brother of James. And He came to the house of Jairus of the synagogue, and saw the great tumult, and all those who wept and wailed greatly. When He came unto the child's bed, He said unto them, "Why make ye this ado, and weep? The damsel is not dead, but sleepeth."

They scorned Him, but He then put them all out, and took the father and the mother of the damsel, and the disciples that were with Him, and took the damsel by the hand and said unto her, "Damsel, I say unto thee, arise."

The little girl of twelve years arose and walked. All there were astonished and joyous. And Jesus charged them strictly that no man should know what had occurred.

Jairus was overjoyed, and unlike so many of the other priests, he knew that this man was to be revered and respected. His wife kneeled before Jesus in gratitude and Jesus said to her, "Arise and get thy daughter something to eat and to drink.

J. Wayne Frye

The Legend of the Fourth Wise Man

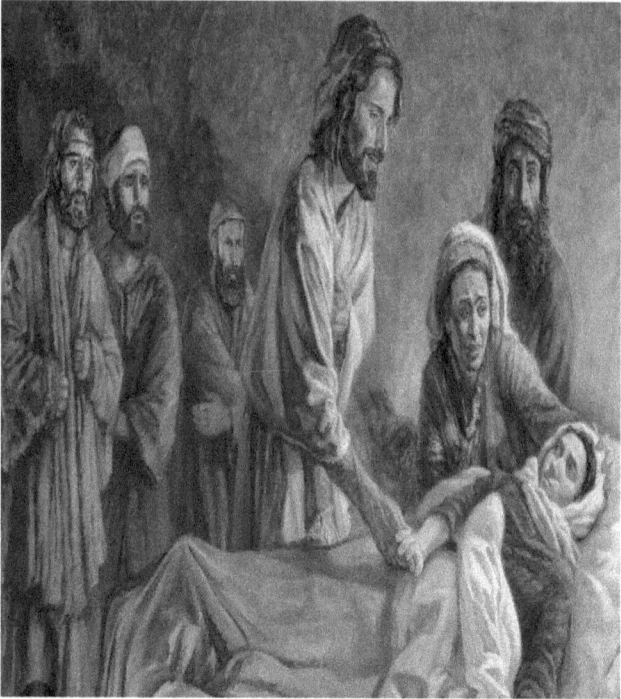

Woodprint (1778) of Jesus raising the dead girl.

Thus was Jesus modest about the miracles He performed. He went out from there, and came into His own country; and His disciples followed Him. And when the Sabbath day came, He began to teach in the synagogue: and many hearing Him were astonished, saying: "From where hath this man got his powers and what wisdom is this which is given unto Him that even such mighty works are wrought by His hands? Is not this the carpenter, the son of Mary, the brother of James and Joses, Juda, and Simon? And are not his sisters here with us, too?"

Thus they were offended at Him for His bold acts. Jesus said, "A prophet is not without honour in his own country, among his own kin and in his own house. He could there do no mighty work, save that he laid his hands upon a few sick folk, and healed them. And he marvelled because of their unbelief."

He went around the villages teaching, calling the twelve, and began to send them forth by two and two; and gave them power over unclean spirits; and commanded them that they should take nothing for their journey, save a staff only; no scrip, no bread, no money in their purse, but be shod with sandals and not put on two coats. And he said unto them, "In what place so ever ye enter into a house, there abide till ye depart from that place. And whosoever shall not receive you, nor hear you, when ye depart thence, shake off the dust under your tired feet for a true testimony against them. Verily I say unto you that it shall be more tolerable for Sodom and Gomorrah in the Day of Judgment, than for that city which boldly rebukes you."

The disciples then went out and spread the word as commanded by Jesus, preaching that

The Legend of the Fourth Wise Man

men should repent. And they cast out many devils, and anointed with oil many that were sick and healed them.

Before long King Herod heard of Him, for his name was spread as tales of his mighty powers were repeated all about the land. Many people proclaimed that He was John-the-Baptist, risen from the dead after being beheaded by Herod at the urging of the teenage temptress, Salome.

When Herod heard thereof, he said with great conviction, "It is John, whom I beheaded. He is raised from the dead."

Herod himself had sent forth and laid hold upon John, and bound him in prison for Herodias' sake, his brother Philip's wife, for he had married her. John had said unto Herod: "It is not lawful for thee to have thy brother's wife." Therefore Herodias had a quarrel against him, and would have killed him; but she could not, for Herod feared John, knowing that he was a just man and considered a holy man. And when a convenient day came that Herod on his birthday made a supper to his lords, high captains and chief nobles of Galilee; and when the daughter of the said Herodias came in, and danced, and pleased Herod and those that sat with him, the king said unto the damsel: "Ask of me whatsoever thou wilt and I will give it thee."

The Legend of the Fourth Wise Man

He swore unto her, "Whatsoever thou shalt ask of me, I will give it thee, unto the half of my kingdom."

And she went forth, and said unto her mother, "What shall I ask?"

And her mother, an equally repulsive human being with no morals, replied, "The head of John the Baptist."

And she came in straightway with haste unto the king, and saying with sinister delight, "I will that thou dear king give me the head of John the Baptist on a platter."

The king was exceedingly sorry; yet for his oath's sake, and for their sakes which sat with him he could not reject her demand as he had given his word. And immediately the king sent an executioner, and commanded John's head to be brought. An executioner was summoned and he immediately went to the dungeon where John was incarcerated and beheaded him. Then he brought his head on a platter, and gave it to the damsel, and the damsel gave it to her mother.

When John's disciples heard of it, they came and took up his corpse, and laid it in a tomb. And, at the time, the apostles gathered

The Legend of the Fourth Wise Man

themselves together unto Jesus, who was a grand admirer of John, and told Him what had happened. Saddened by the news, Jesus hung his head in sorrow.

Yet, he was thoroughly delighted to hear how his disciples had ministered, taught and healed so many in the towns and villages. He told them with renewed conviction, "Come ye yourselves who have served mankind apart into a desert place and rest awhile."

There were many coming and going, and they had no leisure as they departed into a desert place by ship privately. And the people saw them departing, and many knew of Jesus, and ran after Him as He was leaving. Seeing all the people, Jesus was moved with compassion toward them, because they were as sheep not having a shepherd. He stopped and began to teach them great many things about the power of goodness. And when the day was spent, His disciples came unto Him, and said: "This is a desert place, and now the time is far passed. Send them away that they may go into the country round about, and into the villages, and buy themselves bread for they have nothing to eat."

He answered, "Give ye food for them to eat here and now."

The Legend of the Fourth Wise Man

And they said unto Him, "Shall we go and buy two hundred pennyworth of bread and give them that to eat?"

Smiling, Jesus replied, "How many loaves have ye? Go and see."

After checking, the disciples said, "Five and two fishes."

The disciples were perplexed about what Jesus was about to do. They had observed Him performing many miracles, but they still had their doubts about his powers.

Jesus paced about for awhile, stopped and looked to the heavens. He silently prayed. He motioned with outstretched hands and then commanded the disciples to make all sit down upon the green grass. And they sat down in ranks by hundreds and by fifties. All together they numbered maybe 5000 people. And when he had taken the five loaves and the two fishes given him by His disciples, he looked up to heaven, blessed and broke the loaves, and gave them to his disciples to set before them and the two fishes divided he among them all. And they did all eat, and were filled. And they took up twelve baskets full of the fragments of the bread and fishes and the rest of the crowd was then fed with what was left.

J. Wayne Frye

The Legend of the Fourth Wise Man

Woodcut Print (1798)
"The Miracle of the Bread and Fish"

After all had been fed, He ordered His disciples to get into the ship, and to go to the other side unto Bethsaida, while He sent the people away. And when He had sent them away, He departed to a mountain for prayer. And when evening came, the ship was in the midst of the sea, and He alone on the land. He saw them toiling in rowing; for the wind was contrary unto them and about the fourth watch of the night He came to them, walking upon the sea and would have passed by them, but when they saw Him walking upon the sea they

The Legend of the Fourth Wise Man

supposed it a spirit, and cried out for they all saw Him and were troubled. And immediately He talked with them, and said, "Be of good cheer. It is I, be not afraid."

Woodcut Print from 1799
"Jesus Walking on Water"

He went unto them on the ship, and the wind completely ceased, and they were all amazed beyond measure. Despite the many miracles He had performed, they wondered that He had walked on water. Thus, in short order Jesus

The Legend of the Fourth Wise Man

Christ had performed the miracle of the bread and fish and the miracle of walking on water.

They eventually came into the land of Gennesaret and drew to the shore. There, in the towns and villages, people laid the sick in the streets and besought to touch Him or just the border of His garment so they would be healed. They did so and were made whole.

The Legend of the Fourth Wise Man

Chapter 7
Have Peace One with Another

"Verily I say unto you,
Inasmuch as you have done it
to the least of these,
you have done it unto me"

The old man who had been sharing his story of Jesus, seemed wearied, but still Artimus and his companion wanted to hear more, for they were enthralled by these tales of the Christ and how He performed so many miracles. Each tale only wetted their appetites for more details of the man about to be crucified, the man Artimus had been seeking for so long.

The Legend of the Fourth Wise Man

Thus began the continued saga of Christ. It was a weary man who shared the story, but he felt compelled to share what he knew of Jesus.

Then came together unto Him the Pharisees, and certain of the scribes, which came from Jerusalem. And when they saw some of His disciples eat bread with the defiled denizens of the city, and to do so with unwashed hands, they found great fault with Jesus and His followers. (For the Pharisees and all the Jews, wash their hands often. And when they come from the market, they wash cups and pots, brazen vessels and the tables). Then the Pharisees and scribes asked of Jesus "Why walk not thy disciples according to the tradition of the elders, but eat bread with unwashed hands?"

When He entered into a house from the people, His disciples asked him concerning the parable. And he said, "Are ye so without understanding also? Do ye not perceive that whatsoever thing from without entereth into the man it cannot defile him, because it entereth not into his heart, but into the belly, and goeth out into the draught, purging all meats? That which cometh out of the man that defileth the man. For from within, out of the heart of men proceed evil thoughts, adulteries, fornications, murders, thefts, covetousness,

The Legend of the Fourth Wise Man

wickedness, deceit, lasciviousness, an evil eye, blasphemy, pride, foolishness and all these evil things come from within and defile the man."

And then he arose, and went into the borders of Tyre and Sidon, and entered into a house offered for respite and would have no man know it, but he could not be hidden. For a woman, whose young daughter had an unclean spirit, heard of Him and came and fell at His feet. The woman was a Greek, and she sought Him that He would cast forth the devil out of her daughter. But Jesus said unto her: "Let the children first be filled, for it is not meat to take the children's bread and to cast it unto the dogs."

He answered determinedly and said to them with a note of sarcasm in his resonant voice, "Well, hath Esaias prophesied of you hypocrites, as it is written, these people honoureth me with their lips, but their heart is far from me?"

And as they all sat astonished at His boldness, He suddenly called all the people to Him and said, "Hearken unto me every one of you, and understand there is nothing from without a man that enters into him can defile him, but what comes out from the man is what can truly defile him."

The Legend of the Fourth Wise Man

And she answered and said unto him, "Yes, Lord, yet the dogs under the table eat of the children's crumbs."

And he said unto her with great conviction, "For this saying, go thy way; the devil is gone out of thy daughter."

When she came to her house, she found the devil gone out, and her daughter laid upon the bed cured of evil spirits.

Departing from the coasts of Tyre and Sidon, Jesus came unto the sea of Galilee, through the midst of the coasts of Decapolis. And they brought to Him one that was deaf, and had an impediment in his speech, and they beseeched Him to put his hand upon the person. And He took him aside from the multitude, and put His fingers into his ears, and He spit and touched his tongue and looking up to heaven, He sighed unto the man, "Be opened."

The man's ears were opened, and his tongue was loosed, and he spoke plainly. Jesus charged them that they should tell no man: but the more he charged them, so much the more a great deal they made of it and were beyond measure astonished, saying, "He hath done all things well: he maketh both the deaf to hear and the mute to speak."

The Legend of the Fourth Wise Man

He came to Bethsaida, and they brought a blind man unto Him, and besought Him to touch the man. And he took the blind man by the hand, and led him out of the town, and when He had spit on his eyes and put His hands upon the man he asked him if he saw. And he looked up, and said, "I see men as trees, walking."

After that, He put his hands again upon his eyes and made him look up. The man's sight was restored, and he saw every thing clearly. He said of himself that He must suffer many things, and be rejected of the elders, and the chief priests and scribes, and be killed and after three days rise again. Peter began to rebuke him. But when he had turned about and looked on his disciples, He, in turn, rebuked Peter, saying," Get thee behind me Satan, for thou savourest not the things that be of God, but the things that be of men."

He called the people unto Him with his disciples, and said before them all, "Whosoever will come after me, let him deny himself, and take up his cross and follow me. For whosoever will save his life shall lose it; but whosoever shall lose his life for my sake and the gospel's the same shall save it. For what shall it profit a man, if he shall gain the whole world and lose his own soul? Or what shall a man give in

J. Wayne Frye

exchange for his soul? Whosoever, therefore, shall be ashamed of me and of my words in this adulterous and sinful generation of him also shall the son of man be ashamed, when he cometh in the glory of his Father with the holy angels."

"Verily I say unto you my dear brethren that there be some of them that stand here right now, which shall not taste of death till they have seen the kingdom of God come with power."

Jesus went out, with his disciples, into the town of Caesarea Philippi and by the way he asked his disciples, saying unto them: "Who do men say that I am?"

And they answered, "John the Baptist, but some say, Elias; and others one of the prophets."

And Jesus said unto them, "But who say ye that I am?"

Peter answered, "Thou art the Christ."

He charged them that they should be of love for Him, for the time of his death was prescribed. And he began to teach them that the son of man would have to endure suffering.

The Legend of the Fourth Wise Man

And after six days, Jesus took with him Peter, James and John, leading them up into a high mountain apart by themselves, and He was miraculously transfigured before them in a shell of light. And His raiment became shining, exceedingly white as snow; so as nothing fuller on earth could be as white. And there appeared unto them Elias with Moses, and they were talking with Jesus while the disciples looked on in disbelief that two of the most revered prophets has descended upon the mountain.

Peter said to Jesus, "Master, it is good for us to be here: and let us make three tabernacles; one for thee, and one for Moses and one for Elias."

There suddenly was a fluffy cloud that overshadowed them all and a voice came out of the cloud saying, "This is my beloved Son. Hear Him." Suddenly, when they had looked round about, they saw no men there any more, save Jesus only with themselves. And as they came down from the mountain, He charged them that they should tell no man what things they had seen, until the son of man was raised from the dead. Yet, they did not keep the secret, and they kept questioning one another what the rising from the dead should mean.

And they asked him, "Why say the scribes that Elias must first come?"

The Legend of the Fourth Wise Man

He answered to them, "Elias verily cometh first and restoreth all things; and how it is written of the son of man that he must suffer. But I say unto you that Elias is indeed come, and they have done unto him whatsoever was to be done, as it is written of him."

When He returned to his other disciples, He saw a great multitude about them, and the scribes intensely questioning them. And straightway all the people, when they beheld Him, were greatly amazed. He turned to one man and asked the scribe, "What question ye with them?"

He answered, "Master, I have brought unto thee my son, which hath a dumb spirit within him; and whosesoever he taketh him he teareth him, and he foameth, and gnasheth with his teeth, and pineth away and I spake to thy disciples that they should cast out this spirit, but they could not."

Jesus answered him, "Oh faithless generation, how long shall I be with you? How long shall I suffer you? Bring him unto me."

The father had the boy brought unto Him: and when He saw him, straightway the spirit acted within him; and the boy fell on the ground and wallowed, foaming at the mouth.

The Legend of the Fourth Wise Man

Jesus asked his father, "How long is it since this came unto him?"

The father replied, "As a young child. And ofttimes it hath cast him into the fire, and into the waters to destroy him, but if thou can do anything, have compassion on us and help us."

Jesus said unto him, "If thou canst believe, all things are possible to him that believeth."

The father of the child cried out, and said with tears, "Lord, I believe."

When Jesus saw that the people came running together, he rebuked the foul spirit, saying unto it, "Thou dumb and deaf spirit, I charge thee, come out of him, and enter no more into this boy."

The spirit wailed and came out of him. Yet, the boy was as one dead; insomuch, that many there said, "He is dead."

But Jesus took the boy by the hand, and delicately lifted him up. The boy arose. All there were mystified.

When Jesus and the disciples came into the house, His disciples asked him privately, "Why could not we cast out the demon?"

The Legend of the Fourth Wise Man

Jesus said to them, "My faith and belief is greater than yours."

They departed thence and passed through Galilee; and He would not that any man should know it. He said to them," "The son of man is delivered into the hands of men, and they shall kill him; and after that he is killed, he shall rise on the third day."

They did not understand but were afraid to ask Jesus the meaning.

He came to Capernaum: and being in a house He asked them, "What was it that ye disputed among yourselves by the way?" But they held their peace, for they had disputed among themselves who among them after Jesus should be the greatest. And Jesus sat down, and called the twelve to the table.

"If any man desire to be first, the same shall be last of all and servant of all," said a serious Jesus.

He took a child, and sat him in the midst of them, and when he had taken him in His arms, He said unto them, "Whosoever shall receive one of such children in my name, receiveth me: and whosoever shall receive me, receiveth not me, but him that sent me."

The Legend of the Fourth Wise Man

John said, "Master, we saw one casting out devils in thy name, and he followeth not us as we forbade him, because he was not picked by you."

Jesus said, "Forbid him not: for there is no man who shall do a miracle in my name that can lightly speak evil of me. For he that is not against us is on our part. For whosoever shall give you a cup of water to drink in my name, because ye belong to Christ, verily I say unto you he shall not lose his reward. And whosoever shall offend one of these little ones that believe in me, it is better for him that a millstone was hung about his neck, and he was cast into the sea. And if thy hand offend thee, cut it off. It is better for thee to enter into life maimed, than having two hands to go into hell, into the fire that never shall be quenched where their worm dieth not, and the fire is not quenched. And if thy foot offend thee, cut it off. It is better for thee to enter halt into life, than having two feet to be cast into hell, into the fire that never shall be quenched. And if thine eye offend thee, pluck it out. It is better for thee to enter into the kingdom of God with one eye, than having two eyes to be cast into hell fire, where their worm dieth not, and the fire is not quenched. For every one shall be salted with fire, and every sacrifice shall be salted with salt. Salt is good, but if the salt has lost his saltiness,

The Legend of the Fourth Wise Man

wherewith will ye season it? Have salt in yourselves and have peace one with another."

The Legend of the Fourth Wise Man

Chapter 8
Seal His Fate

When Jesus had fed the five thousand and more,
Who'd witnessed the signs of His healing before;
They said He was truly the Prophet foretold;
Their active response grew increasingly bold.

A popular movement was starting to build;
Their longing for freedom could now be fulfilled;
The Roman oppressors had taken the reins;
A captain was needed to break off the chains.

But Jesus could see their intentions were wrong;
He would not be moved by a popular throng;
He knew they were fickle as human can be;

J. Wayne Frye

The Legend of the Fourth Wise Man

Political fervour is never the key.

He went by Himself to a mountain to pray;
He needed this time in the stress of the day;
His closer disciples had boarded a boat,
But soon they were struggling to keep it afloat.

A storm broke upon them; a tempest severe;
The Lord came and quietened their fear;
The people took shipping across in their wake,
They didn't know Jesus had walked on the lake.

They sought Him as soon as they got to the land;
When did you come here was their demand;
He knew they were taking a practical line,
Content with the food after seeing the sign.

So Jesus recalled the events of the day,
Of work that is mortal and passing away;
Their labour should be for the food that endures,
The gift of the Father and what it secures.

The people were missing the object in sight;
They thought there was merit in doing right;
But Jesus rejected their singular bent;
Their focus must be on the One who is sent.

They asked for a sign of what Jesus could do,
That they might believe and accept Him as true;
Our fathers ate manna, and so did they quote;
Presenting this factor as worthy of note.

J. Wayne Frye 106

The Legend of the Fourth Wise Man

But Jesus corrected their Scriptural view;
My Father is giving the true bread to you;
They said to Him, Lord, give this bread evermore;
As yet not discerning the Person they saw.

He gave further light to what Scripture had said,
Your fathers ate manna but now they are dead;
Whoever partakes of the bread that I give,
Shall never see death but eternally live.

The bread is My flesh and the drink is My blood;
The terms that He stated were misunderstood;
For many who heard were overtly dismayed;
They could not accept this assertion He made.

When Jesus perceived they murmured at this;
That what He was teaching was taken amiss,
He made an appeal to His future ascent,
For that was the key to His whole argument.

The Spirit gives life but the flesh profits naught;
The words I speak are spiritually taught;
But there are among you who do not believe;
For one would betray Him as He could perceive.

Many turned back and went with Him no more;
For Jesus had stated an unwritten law:
That no one can come to the true Son of Man,
Excepting the Father has granted he can.

The Lord is our manna and heavenly bread;

J. Wayne Frye

The Legend of the Fourth Wise Man

The gift of the Father as Scripture has said;
Our soul will be nourished whatever the need,
As filled with the Spirit on Jesus we feed.

Suddenly, a vast throng of people came down the road and Artimus asked one of them where they were headed. He replied, "We go to Golgotha, where the man Jesus is to be crucified. He will be making his way there, carrying his cross on these very streets. Pontius Pilot has already sentenced him. "

Bowing his head, the man sitting on the steps said to Artimus and Rachael, "Go if you want, but I shall not, as I do not want to see an innocent man suffer this abomination. He has done no wrong, but those with power see him as a threat, a threat to their privileged positions which they have because they keep the people in ignorance. These arrogant privileged ones depend on a compliant populace that is easily turned astray by hypocrites. Yet, there are those moving toward Golgotha now that are not as easily swayed as are the others who are complacent in this abomination. Those who refuse to see evil have become a part of the evil. This is the way of a world where evil masquerades as good under the guise of religion. Religion is more about control than anything else, and this man Jesus calls it out and deplores it."

The Legend of the Fourth Wise Man

Artimus said, "We will wait for this man Jesus and follow him to Golgotha when he comes by."

The stranger replied, "He will be by here before long, for He is not far behind me." The stranger turned and walked up the road among the throng headed to Golgotha.

Artimus said to the man on the steps, "Please continue with your story."

The man did, telling more of the glories of Jesus. He told of how Jesus went to the coasts of Judaea by the farther side of the Jordan and the people assembled unto Him again; and He taught them once more. And the Pharisees came to him, and asked him, "Is it lawful for a man to put away his wife," as they were tempting him.

Jesus replied, "What did Moses command you?"

And they said, "Moses suffered to write a bill of divorcement and to put the woman away."

Jesus said unto them, "For the hardness of your heart he wrote you this precept. But from the beginning of the creation, God made them male and female. For this cause shall a man leave his father and mother, and cleave to his wife, and they twain shall be one flesh, so then they are no more twain. What therefore God hath joined together, let not man put asunder."

And in the house, his disciples asked him again of the same matter. He said unto them, "Whosoever shall put away his wife and marry another committeth adultery against her. And if a woman shall put away her husband, and be married to another, she committeth adultery."

They brought young children to him that he should touch them, and his disciples rebuked those that brought them. But when Jesus saw it, he was much displeased, and said unto them, "Suffer the little children to come unto me, and forbid them not for of such is the kingdom of God. Verily I say unto you. Whosoever shall not receive the kingdom of God as a little child, he shall not enter therein."

The Legend of the Fourth Wise Man

Jesus took the little children up in his arms, put his loving hands upon them and blessed them.

When the children were gone forth from Him, there came one person franticly running up to Jesus. The person kneeled and asked, "Good Master, what shall I do that I may inherit eternal life?"

Jesus said unto him, "Why callest thou me good? There is none good but one, that is God. Thou knowest the commandments, Do not commit adultery. Do not kill. 'Do not steal. Do not bear false witness. Defraud not and honour thy father and mother.'"

The man replied unto him, "Master, all these have I observed from my youth."

Then Jesus, beholding him loved him and said, "One thing thou lackest. Go thy way, sell whatsoever thou hast, and give to the poor and thou shalt have treasure in heaven. Take up the cross and follow me."

The man was saddened at that saying and went away grieved for he had great possessions. Jesus looked round about, and said unto his disciples, "How hardly shall they that have riches enter into the kingdom of God!"

The Legend of the Fourth Wise Man

And the disciples were astonished. But Jesus said unto them, "Children, how hard is it for them that trust in riches to enter into the kingdom of God! It is easier for a camel to go through the eye of a needle, than for a rich man to enter into the kingdom of God."

And they were astonished out of measure, saying among themselves, "Who then can be saved?"

Jesus, looking upon them, said, "With men it is impossible, but not with God, for with God all things are possible."

Then Peter began to say unto him, "Lo, we have left all and have followed thee."

And Jesus said, "Verily I say unto you. There is no man that hath left house, or brethren, or sisters, or father, or mother, or wife, or children, or lands for my sake and the gospel's, but he shall receive a hundredfold now in this time, houses and brethren, and sisters, and mothers, and children, and lands, with persecutions; and in the world to come eternal life. But many that are first shall be last; and the last first."

They were now going up to Jerusalem, and Jesus went before them. They were amazed as

The Legend of the Fourth Wise Man

they followed. They were afraid. And he took again the twelve and began to tell them what things should happen unto Him, saying, "Behold, we go up to Jerusalem and the Son of man shall be delivered unto the chief priests, and unto the scribes, and they shall condemn Him to death and shall deliver Him to the Gentiles. They shall mock Him and shall scourge Him, and shall spit upon Him and shall kill Him and the third day He shall rise again."

James and John, sons of Zebedee, came unto him, saying, "We would that thou shouldest do for us whatsoever we shall desire."

He said unto them, "What would ye that I should do for you?"

They said unto Him, "Grant unto us that we may sit, one on thy right hand and the other on thy left hand in thy glory."

But Jesus said unto them, "Ye know not what ye ask. Can ye drink of the cup that I drink of and be baptized with the baptism that I am baptized with?"

They said unto him, "We can."

Jesus said unto them, "Ye shall indeed drink of the cup that I drink of and with the baptism

The Legend of the Fourth Wise Man

that I am baptized withal shall ye be baptized, but to sit on my right hand and on my left hand is not mine to give; but it shall be given to them for whom it is prepared."

When the ten others heard it, they began to be much displeased with James and John, but Jesus called them to Him and said, "Ye know that they which are accounted to rule over the Gentiles exercise lordship over them and their great ones exercise authority upon them. But so shall it not be among you, but whosoever will be great among you shall be your minister and whosoever of you will be the chiefest shall be servant of all. For even the son of man came not to be ministered unto, but to minister and to give his life as ransom for many."

Then they came to Jericho, and as He went out of Jericho with his disciples and a great number of people blind Bartimaeus sat by the highway side begging. And when he heard that it was Jesus of Nazareth, he began to cry out and say, "Jesus, thou son of David, have mercy on me."

Many charged the blind man that he should hold his peace, but he cried the more a great deal, "Thou son of David, have mercy on me."

Jesus stood still, and commanded him to be called. And they called the blind man, saying

The Legend of the Fourth Wise Man

unto him, "Be of good comfort, rise; he calleth thee."

And he, casting away his garment, rose, and came to Jesus.

Jesus answered and said unto him, "What wilt thou that I should do unto thee?"

The blind man said unto him, "Lord, that I might receive my sight."

Jesus said unto him, "Go thy way; thy faith hath made thee whole." And immediately he received his sight.

Abstract Art - Jesus Making the Blind See

J. Wayne Frye

The Legend of the Fourth Wise Man

When they came to Jerusalem, unto Bethphage and Bethany, at the mount of Olives, He sent forth two of his disciples, and said unto them, "Go your way into the village over against you and as soon as ye be entered into it ye shall find a donkey tied, whereon never man sat. Loose him and bring him here. And if any man asks why do ye this say to him that The Lord hath need of him and straightway he will send him hither."

They went their way and found the donkey tied by the door without in a place where two ways met and they loosed him. And certain of them that stood there said unto them, "What do ye loosen the donkey?" And they said unto as Jesus had commanded, and they let them go. And they brought the donkey to Jesus, and cast their garments on him; and he sat upon the donkey. And many spread their garments in the way and others cut down branches off the trees, and strew them in the way. And they that went before and they that followed, cried, saying, "Hosanna, blessed is he that cometh in the name of the Lord. Blessed be the kingdom of our father David, that cometh in the name of the Lord - Hosanna in the highest."

And Jesus entered into Jerusalem on the back of that donkey as people laid garments and tree branches on the ground before Him.

J. Wayne Frye 116

The Legend of the Fourth Wise Man

Woodcut: Jesus Entering Jerusalem

The next day they came to Jerusalem again. Jesus went into the temple, casting out those that sold and bought there, and overthrew tables of the money changers, and the seats of them that sold doves and would not suffer that any man should carry any vessel through the temple. And He taught, saying unto them, 'My house shall be called of all nations the house of prayer?' But ye have made it a den of thieves."

The Legend of the Fourth Wise Man

*Old rendering of Jesus chasing
out the money changers from the temple.*

The scribes and chief priests heard about it, and sought how they might destroy Him, for they feared Him greatly, because all the people were astonished at His doctrine and wise counsel. However, as they plotted against Him. Jesus went out of the city.

On the way they passed by a dried up fig tree. And Peter calling, said unto Jesus, "Master, behold, the fig tree is withered away."

The Legend of the Fourth Wise Man

Jesus said, "Have faith in God. For verily I say unto you, that whosoever shall say unto this mountain, be removed and be thou cast into the sea and shall not doubt in his heart, but shall believe that those things which he saith shall come to pass. He shall have whatsoever he saith. Therefore, I say unto you what things so ever ye desire, when ye pray, believe that ye receive them, and ye shall have them. And when ye stand praying, forgive; if ye have ought against any that your Father also which is in heaven may forgive you your trespasses. But if ye do not forgive, neither will your Father, which is in heaven, forgive your trespasses."

The next day they came again to Jerusalem, and as Jesus was walking in the temple, there came to Him the chief priests, the scribes, and the elders, and said unto Him: "By what authority doest thou these things and who gave thee this authority to do these things?"

Jesus said unto them with great conviction and concern, "I will also ask of you one question and answer me, and I will tell you by what authority I do these things. The baptism of John, was it from heaven or of men? Answer me."

They, fearing the reaction of Jesus and the crowd said, "We cannot tell."

The Legend of the Fourth Wise Man

Jesus said unto them, "Neither do I tell you by what authority I do these things."

They sought to lay hold on him, but feared the people, for they knew that He had riled the people against them. So, they left Him and went their way. Yet, they took their deceit with them and planned treachery.

They sent unto Him certain of the Pharisees and of the Herodians to catch Him in His words. When they came, they said unto Him, "Master, we know that thou art true, and carest for no man for thou regardest not the person of men but teachest the way of God in truth. Is it lawful to give tribute to Caesar, or not? Shall we give, or shall we not give?"

Knowing their hypocrisy, He said, "Why tempt ye me? Bring me a penny that I may see it."

They brought him a penny, and He said, "Whose is this image and superscription?"

They said unto him, "Caesar's."

And Jesus answering said unto them, "Render to Caesar the things that are Caesar's, and to God the things that are God's."

They marvelled at him.

The Legend of the Fourth Wise Man

Then come unto him the Sadducees, which say there is no resurrection and they asked him, "Master, Moses wrote unto us that if a man's brother die and leaves his wife behind and leaves no children that his brother should take his wife and raise up seed unto his brother. Now there were seven brethren and the first took a wife, and dying left no seed. And the second took her, and died, neither left he any seed. The third likewise. And the seven had her and left no seed. Last of all, the woman died also. In the resurrection therefore, when they shall rise, whose wife shall she be of them, for the seven had her to wife?"

Jesus said unto them, "Do ye not therefore err, because ye know not the scriptures, neither the power of God? For when they shall rise from the dead, they neither marry, nor are given in marriage; but are as the angels which are in heaven. And as touching the dead that they rise have ye not read in the book of Moses, how in the bush God spake unto him, saying, 'I am the God of Abraham, and the God of Isaac, and the God of Jacob?' He is not the God of the dead, but the God of the living. You greatly err."

One of the scribes came, and having heard the reasoning, and perceiving that he had answered them well, asked Him, "Which is the first commandment of all?"

The Legend of the Fourth Wise Man

Jesus answered, "The first of all the commandments is, Hear, O Israel; The Lord our God is one Lord and thou shalt love the Lord thy God with all thy heart and with all thy soul, and with all thy mind, and with all thy strength. This is the first commandment."

He continued, "The second is Thou shalt love thy neighbour as thyself. There are no other commandments greater than these."

The scribe verily said unto Him, "Well, Master, thou hast said the truth, for there is one God and there is none other but he and to love Him with all the heart, and with all the understanding, and with all the soul, and with all the strength, and to love his neighbour as himself, is more than all whole burnt offerings and sacrifices."

Jesus said to him with respect, "Thou art not far from the kingdom of God."

The common people heard Him gladly, and he said unto them, "Beware of the scribes, which love to go in long clothing, love salutations in the market places, and take the chief seats in the synagogues, and the uppermost rooms at feasts: which devour widows' houses, and for a pretence make long prayers. These shall receive greater damnation."

The Legend of the Fourth Wise Man

Jesus sat over against the treasury, and beheld how the people cast money into the treasury. Many that were rich cast in much. And there came a certain poor widow, and she threw in two mites, which make a farthing. And he called unto him His disciples, and said "Verily I say unto you, that this poor widow hath cast more in, than all they which have cast into the treasury, for all they did cast in of their abundance, but she cast in all that she had, even all her living. This is a true servant to God."

Jesus' final teaching in the temple

J. Wayne Frye

The Legend of the Fourth Wise Man

Thus, on this day was the final dramatic teaching that would seal His fate!

The Legend of the Fourth Wise Man

Chapter 9
He Wept

And did those feet in ancient time,
Walk upon mountains green,
And was the holy Lamb of God,
On pleasant pastures seen!

And did the Countenance Divine,
Shine forth upon clouded hills?
And was Jerusalem built there,
Among those dark sided hills?

Bring me my bow of burning gold.
Bring me my arrows of desire.
Bring me my spear and clouds unfold.

J. Wayne Frye

The Legend of the Fourth Wise Man

Bring me my chariot of fire!

I will not cease from mental fight,
Nor shall my sword sleep in my hand,
Till we have built Jerusalem,
Into a green & pleasant Land.

Taking a deep breath and looking into the eyes of Artimus, the old man turned and gazed down the street, saw the crowds coming their way, and he hurried with the rest of his tale.

All but one of the scribes was determined to make an example of Jesus. For his questioning the order of things as they had been for so long was unacceptable. They huddled and plotted as Jesus left the temple.

Outside the temple, one of the disciples said to Him, "Master, see what manner of stones and what buildings are here!"

Jesus answering said, "Seest thou these great buildings? There shall not be left one stone upon another that shall not be thrown down."

As He sat upon the Mount of Olives over against the temple, Peter, James, John and Andrew asked him privately, "Tell us, when shall these things be, and what shall be the sign when all these things be fulfilled?"

The Legend of the Fourth Wise Man

Jesus said, "Lest any man deceive you, for many shall come in my name, saying, I am Christ and shall deceive many. And when ye shall hear of wars and rumours of wars, be ye not troubled, for such things must be, but the end shall not be yet. For nation shall rise against nation, and kingdom against kingdom, and there shall be earthquakes in diverse places, and there shall be famines and troubles. These are the beginnings of sorrows. But take heed to yourselves, for they shall deliver you up to councils, and in the synagogues ye shall be beaten and ye shall be brought before rulers and kings for my sake. And the gospel must first be published among all nations. But when they shall lead you, and deliver you up, take no thought beforehand what ye shall speak, neither do ye premeditate, but whatsoever shall be given you in that hour it is not ye that speak but the Holy Ghost. Now the brother shall betray the brother to death, and the father the son, and children shall rise up against their parents and shall cause them to be put to death. And ye shall be hated of all men for my name's sake, but he that shall endure unto the end, the same shall be saved. But when ye shall see the abomination of desolation, spoken of by Daniel the prophet, standing where it ought not, then let them that be in Judaea flee to the mountains and let him that is on the housetop not go down into the house, neither enter therein, to take

J. Wayne Frye   127

The Legend of the Fourth Wise Man

any thing out of his house and let him that is in the field not turn back again for to take up his garment. For in those days shall be affliction, such as was not from the beginning of the creation which God created unto this time. And then if any man shall say to you, 'Lo, here is Christ;' or, 'lo, he is there;' believe him not, for false Christs and false prophets shall rise and shall sew signs and wonders, to seduce. But take ye heed: behold, I have foretold you all things that will occur before the end."

Artimus then asked the old man, as the crowd neared, what Jesus said about the end of days? The old man said that the sun shall be darkened, and the moon not give her light, and the stars of heaven shall fall and the powers that are in heaven shall be shaken. They shall see the Son of Man coming in the clouds with great power and glory. And then shall he send his angels, and shall gather together his elect from the four winds, from the uttermost part of the earth to the uttermost part of heaven.

He further told that all needed to learn the parable of the fig tree as when her branch is yet tender, and puts forth leaves, ye know that summer is near. So ye, in like manner, when ye shall see these things come to pass, know that it is nigh, even at the doors. It is then that heaven and earth shall pass away, but His words shall not pass away. But of that day and that hour knows no man. No, not the angels which are in heaven, neither the Son, but only the Father does. Watch ye therefore, for ye know not when the master of the house cometh, at eveningtide, or at midnight, or at the cock-crowing or in the morning.

At this point, our story must have some specific clarification outside what happened between Artimus and the old man. It so happens that two days after Jesus left the scribes dumbfounded with his parables there was the feast of the Passover, and of unleavened bread, and the chief priests and the scribes sought how they might take him by craft, and put him to death. But they said, "Not on the feast day, lest there be an uproar of the people."

And being in Bethany in the house of Simon the leper, as He sat at the table, there came a woman having an alabaster box of ointment of spikenard, very precious; and she broke the box and poured it on Jesus' head. And there were some that had indignation within themselves, and said, "Why was this waste of the ointment made? For it might have been sold for more than three hundred pence, and have been given to the poor." And they murmured against her.

The Legend of the Fourth Wise Man

Jesus said, "Let her alone; why trouble ye her? She hath wrought a good work on me. For ye have the poor with you always, and when so ever ye will ye may do them good, but me ye have not always. She hath done what she could. She is come to anoint my body for the burying. Verily I say unto you, where so ever this gospel shall be preached throughout the whole world, this also that she hath done shall be spoken of for a memorial of her."

Judas Iscariot, one of the twelve apostles, went unto the chief priests to betray Jesus unto them. And when they heard from him, they were glad, and promised to give him money. And he sought how he might conveniently betray Jesus.

On the first day of unleavened bread, the disciples said unto Jesus, "Where wilt thou that we go and prepare that thou mayest eat the Passover?"

He sent forth two of his disciples, and said unto them, "Go ye into the city, and there shall meet you a man bearing a pitcher of water. Follow him and where so ever he shall go in ask where the guest chamber is where the Master shall eat the Passover with His disciples? He will show you a large upper room furnished and prepared. There make ready for us."

The Legend of the Fourth Wise Man

His disciples went forth, and came into the city, and found as he had said unto them, and they made ready the Passover. And in the evening Jesus communed with the twelve. And as they sat and ate, Jesus said, "Verily I say unto you, one of you which eateth with me shall betray me."

They began to be sorrowful, and to say unto Him one by one, "Is it I?" and another said, "Is it I?"

He answered and said unto them, "It is one of the twelve that dippeth with me in the dish. The Son of Man indeed goeth, as it is written of him, but woe to that man by whom the Son of Man is betrayed! Good were it for that man if he had never been born."

As they did eat, Jesus took bread, and blessed, and broke it and gave to them saying, "Take, eat. This is my body."

He reverently and with great care took the cup, and when he had given thanks, he gave it to them: and they all drank of it. And he said unto them, "This is my blood of the new testament, which is shed for many. Verily I say unto you, I will drink no more of the fruit of the vine, until that day that I drink it new in the kingdom of God."

The Legend of the Fourth Wise Man

When they had sung a hymn, they went out into the Mount of Olives. And Jesus said unto them, "All ye shall be offended because of me this night. For it is written, 'I will smite the shepherd, and the sheep shall be scattered.' But after that I am risen, I will go before you into Galilee."

Peter said unto him, "Although all shall be offended, yet will not I."

Jesus said unto him, "Verily I say unto thee, that this day, even in this night, before the cock crows twice, thou shalt deny me thrice."

Peter spoke more vehemently, "If I should die with thee, I will not deny thee."

Likewise, said they all. Though they meant it at the time, they would betray him.

They came to a place which was named Gethsemane, and Jesus said to his disciples, "Sit ye here, while I shall pray." And He took with him Peter, James and John, and began to be amazed and to be very heavy in sorrow; and said unto them, "My soul is exceeding sorrowful unto death. Tarry ye here, and watch."

Jesus went forward a little, fell on the ground, and prayed that if it were possible the hour might pass from Him. He said, "Abba, Father, all things are possible unto thee; take away this cup from me; nevertheless, not what I will, but what thou wilt."

He found the disciples sleeping, and said unto Peter, "Simon, sleepest thou? Couldest not thou watch one hour? Watch ye and pray, lest ye enter into temptation. The spirit truly is ready, but the flesh is weak."

"Sleep now, take each your rest. It is enough, the hour is come; behold, the Son of Man is betrayed into the hands of sinners. Rise up, let us go; lo, he that betrayeth me is at hand."

Immediately, while He yet spoke, cometh Judas Iscariot, one of the twelve, and with him a great multitude with swords and staves, from the chief priests and the scribes and the elders. And he that betrayed Him had given them a token, saying, "Whomsoever I shall kiss, that same is He; take Him, and lead Him away safely."

As soon as Judas came, he went straightway to Jesus, and said, "Master, master;" and kissed him on the cheek.

Peter drew his sword and cut off the ear of Malchus, the high priest's servant. Jesus

The Legend of the Fourth Wise Man

rebuked Peter for this, reached up, placed his hand over the man's ear and it was healed. Jesus further said to those abducting Him: "Are ye come out, as against a thief, with swords and with staves to take me? I was daily with you in the temple teaching, and ye took me not, but the scriptures must be fulfilled."

They led Jesus away to the high priest, and with him were assembled all the chief priests, the elders and scribes. Peter followed him, even into the palace of the high priest. He sat and warmed himself at the fire. The chief priests and council sought witnesses against Jesus to put him to death. Then there arose certain ones to bare false witness against him, saying, "We heard him say, 'I will destroy this temple that is made with hands, and within three days I will build another made without hands."

The high priest stood and pointedly asked Jesus, "Answerest thou nothing? What is it which these witness against thee?"

Jesus held his peace and answered not. Again the high priest asked him, "Art thou the Christ, the Son of the Blessed?"

Jesus replied, "I am and ye shall see the Son of man sitting on the right hand of power and coming in the clouds of heaven."

The Legend of the Fourth Wise Man

Then the high priest said, "What need we any further witnesses? Ye have heard the blasphemy. What think ye?" And they all condemned him to be guilty. And some began to spit on him, to cover his face and to buffet him.

As Peter was beneath in the palace, there came one of the maids of the high priest. When she saw Peter warming himself, she looked upon him, and said, "And thou also wast with Jesus of Nazareth."

But he denied, saying, "I know not, neither understand I what thou sayest." And he went out into the porch; and the cock crew.

A maid saw him again, and began to say to them that stood by, "This is one of them."

He denied it again. And a little after, they that stood by said again to Peter, "Surely thou art one of them, for thou art a Galilean."

Then he began to curse heartily and to swear, saying, "I know not this man of whom ye speak."

Thus, the second time the cock crew. And Peter called to mind the word that Jesus said unto him, "Before the cock crow twice, thou shalt deny me thrice." And when he thought thereon, he wept.

The Legend of the Fourth Wise Man

Chapter 10
King of the Jews

The sun, a cruel eye, beats on the hill,
Casting long shadows, fear and chill.
A man stands; gaze fixed and heart a-thrum,
At the sight of Jesus, burdened and numb.

Wood, rough and splintered, groaning low,
Holds limbs outstretched, a painful show.
The crown of thorns, a cruel design,
Marks a brow where grace should brightly shine.

He sees the blood, a crimson tear,
From hands and feet, a vision clear.
A sacrifice, a heavy price,

The Legend of the Fourth Wise Man

Paid for the world in bitter vice.

The man's own sins, a heavy chain,
Seem light beside this piercing pain.
He feels the pull, the desperate plea,
Of love and loss, for all to see.

A silent promise, in that gaze,
Of hope reborn, in coming days.
A future won, beyond the wood,
If only faith is understood.

The man turns, changed, with heavy tread,
To face the world, no longer dead.
For in that cross, a truth he found,
A love that saves on holy ground.

Then, the crowd came blistering down the street, following Jesus, who was bearing His own cross, because the chief priests, hypocrites just like so many hypocrites in the synagogues and churches then and today, had bound Jesus and carried Him away where they held council with the elders and the scribes and delivered him unto Pontius Pilate, the governor of Judea.

When Pilate had asked if He was the king of Jews, Jesus' reply was, "Thou sayest it."

The chief priests accused Him of many things, but He answered nothing. And Pilate asked Him again, saying, "Answerest thou nothing? Behold how many things they witness against thee."

Jesus answered nothing, so that Pilate marvelled. One prisoner was to be granted clemency with Pilate releasing whomsoever the crowd desired. And there was one named Barabbas, which lay bound with Jesus and others, who had committed insurrection. And the multitude crying aloud began to desire Barabbas to be freed.

Pilate answered their plea, saying, "Will ye not let me release unto you the King of the Jews?" For he knew that the chief priests had delivered him out of envy. But the chief priests moved the people to demand the release of Barabbas.

Pilate answered and said again unto them, "What will ye then that I shall do unto Him who ye call the King of the Jews?"

They cried out, "Crucify him."

Then Pilate said unto them, "Why, what evil hath he done?"

And they cried out more exceedingly, "Crucify him." Pilate, willing to content the people, released Barabbas unto them and delivered

The Legend of the Fourth Wise Man

Jesus, when he had scourged him, to be crucified.

The soldiers led him away into the hall and they clothed Him with purple, platted a crown of thorns, put it about his head and began to salute him, "Hail, King of the Jews!"

They smote Him on the head with a reed, spit upon Him, and bowing their knees mockingly worshipped Him. They then took off the purple, put His own clothes on Him and led Him out to be crucified. Thus, he was now passing by Artimus, who had sought this man for so many years.

Passing by Artimus, Jesus turned His head and looked up at him with penetrating, suffering eyes. Artimus was dumbstruck and could say nothing, only look in desperation as Jesus walked up the road to Golgotha. Artimus, gesturing goodbye to the old man on the steps, walked with the woman up the road, following Jesus. They stood in misery watching Jesus being nailed to the cross.

They watched in dismay as the crucifiers parted His garments, casting lots upon them over what each individual should take. Over His head was written the words *The King of the Jews.*

Chapter 11
A Precious Thing

Saving Love on Holy Ground
(The Power of the Cross)

The sun, a cruel eye, beats on the hill,
Casting long shadows, fear and chill.
A man stands, gaze fixed, and heart a-thrum,
At the sight of Jesus, burdened, numb.

Wood, rough and splintered, groaning low,
Holds limbs outstretched, a painful show.
The crown of thorns, a cruel design,
Marks a brow where grace should brightly shine.

He sees the blood, a crimson tear,
From hands and feet, a vision clear.

J. Wayne Frye   141

The Legend of the Fourth Wise Man

A sacrifice, a heavy price,
Paid for the world, in bitter vice.

The man's own sins, a heavy chain,
Seem light beside this piercing pain.
He feels the pull, the desperate plea,
Of love and loss, for all to see.

A silent promise, in that gaze,
Of hope reborn in coming days.
A future won, beyond the wood,
If only faith is understood.

The man turns, changed, with heavy tread,
To face the world, no longer dead.
For in that cross, a truth he found,
A love that saves on holy ground.

Artimus, weary and exhausted now, after 33 years of searching, had found that king he had sought for so long. He collapsed onto the ground, and he breathed a sigh of relief, but felt he had failed, for he only found the saviour when he was on the cross. Yet, he was about to realize that success is not final, and that failure is not fatal. It is the courage to continue that counts. And Artimus had continued for 33 years in search of that king born to bring salvation to all of mankind. Truth is no great success was ever achieved without failure. It may be one epic failure or a series of failures.

The Legend of the Fourth Wise Man

Artimus had failed time and time again in his quest, but in doing so he had actually succeeded in helping many others along the way in his many travels. Helping others was actually the greatest gift of all he could have given to Jesus, who gave His life on the cross for all humanity. Jesus bowed his head and looked down at Artimus lying on the ground in Rachael's arms. In those eyes Artimus saw love and appreciation for his commitment.

He was held by his companion as he looked up at Jesus on the cross. He needed not say a word, because in Jesus' countenance, Artimus knew he had finally fulfilled his goal of honouring the king.

He found the Jesus being crucified inside the wall.
Going to see the King, the walls on would fall.
As he lay dying, he looked up into Jesus' face,
And felt the joy of the Lord's redeeming embrace.

Artimus said "Oh King I've nothing to give to you.
I had precious stones, but they are gone, too!"
Jesus said to him, "You gave all to me,
For you gave to others, so they might be free!"

This is the beautiful tale of the other wise man,
Who in compassion for others took a stand.
In doing so, he gave his gifts unto the King,
Which in the Lord's mind was a precious thing.

J. Wayne Frye   143

The Legend of the Fourth Wise Man

*Illustration of Artimus as he died
in the shadow of the cross. (Woodcut 1765)*

The Legend of the Fourth Wise Man

Epilogue
As My Grandmother Would Say

Scratch the surface of joy,
And you will find a well of sorrow.
Dive into the well,
And discover a spring of hope.
Follow that spring with a river of compassion,
And you will have touched a soul.

I am not a person of great faith, but I see the circle of life and try to do good, as the fourth wise man did consistently, and it interfered with his quest to honour Jesus just as my quest to do good has often led me to great heartache and turmoil. Yet, I know of no other way to face

J. Wayne Frye 145

The Legend of the Fourth Wise Man

life, for I have always believed in the power of good.

I had a grandmother who once told me that when a bird is alive it eats ants. When the bird dies, ants eat it. She said that time and circumstances change things. Thus, do not devalue or hurt anyone in life. You may be powerful today, but remember that time is more powerful than you are. One tree can make a million matches, but it only takes one match to burn a million trees.

The fourth wise man is forgotten in history, but his dedication and devotion was recognized by Jesus; consequently, *always be aware of karma and be good and do good*, as my grandmother would say!

The End

Other Jesus books by J. Wayne Frye : available at on-line retailers and all major bookstores

When Jesus Came to Jersey as the Son of Thunder

When Jesus Came to Canada to Lead an Indigenous Rebellion in the Broughton Archipelago

When Jesus Came to the Black Hills to do the Ghost Dance with the Resurrected Spirit Of Sitting Bull

When Jesus Came to Ladysmith to Battle The Angel of Death

J. Wayne Frye

www.ingramcontent.com/pod-product-compliance
Lightning Source LLC
Chambersburg PA
CBHW060508030426
42337CB00015B/1796